Salvation Through Yourself

WATARASE
Vol. 2

Kazuyo Omori

たま出版

Prologue

The luxury of free time

*To have the freedom of time, and to be able to use time
for yourself, is the greatest luxury in this world.
Unless you enjoy this precious time, all is wasted.
Nobody is there to control your time, oppressing and
commanding you to do anything.
To have such free time is, in other words, a blessing from God.
Many receive this blessing after retirement
at the ending of one's life.
To regard this time as lonesome, boring without much to do, or
loathing for the physical incapability, waiting for the end to
come, all is up to you.
However, when your life is being closed after having worked
hard in your own way,
we wish you to spend this time looking back at your life and
reflecting in tranquility.
Reflect where need to be done, and challenge all not done . . .
We want you to spend this luxurious time enjoying yourself
in your own way, and make your life full.
We are not preaching anything complicated.
We just want you to have as much fun as you can.
Our dearest . . .*

This is a message I have received from a god as a spiritual counselor.

In recent years, deaths of isolated individuals and society with no connections have been the focus of the media. People's relations with society and family bondage have become weaker, and the situation where many people died lonely deaths has received great attention.

You may feel pity for those who have passed away lonely without anybody present. As seen in the opening message, however, a god says: "A solitary death is not necessarily unfortunate. A man's happiness is to have the freedom of time." Among those who have died alone, there are some who openly enjoyed life's precious gift of freedom.

Those who have died without being attended by anyone at home are generally treated as people who died unnatural death, and later they are likely to become earthbound spirits. However, that is only true of young people. In the case that the elderly pass away as if asleep, according to a god, they may not become earthbound spirits only because they happen to be discovered later. That is, even in the case treated as solitary death, they themselves die in peace and leave for the Astral Realm.

The other day when I was watching TV, on the screen I saw the spirit of the deceased man who seemed to be over 80 years old. He was reported to have died alone without anybody knowing but did not seem to be in any agony. I asked a god, "Is he an earthbound spirit?" The god replied: "He is not an earthbound spirit. Although he did not have others to rely upon, he was able to live happily on his own, doing what he desired until the last moments of his life. Upon reaching the 49th day after death, he will be able to receive his divine judgment."

Those who are living on their own right now may be feeling restless every day. However, I think that you should just enjoy this time in your own way. This does not mean that you should spend your money a lot to enjoy yourselves. For example, you can look back and reflect on your life, or maybe start to keep a diary. If it is hard for you to write by hand, you can record your voice in a recorder. In this way, you can document how your days on your own are through words and voices.

By leaving your emotions as words or as a recording, you may feel much better. Moreover, your words could be left to be read or listened to by the people of the future generations. This could be a form to document your life. In this way, people can understand that those living on their own do not necessarily feel miserable. Understanding the feeling of the elderly living alone may consequently lead people to change the views on them, and get to know how to deal with them. This also could be a way to "help others" or to "live for others".

I published *WATARASE: The way to your higher self* (Tama

Publishing) in March 2010, which had a greater response than I had expected. In my book, I wrote about my unusual childhood experiences as well as the spiritual existences and the importance to elevate the soul, and introduced some words from gods. I was informed by the publisher that, for a book including spiritual messages, it has been enjoying an unusually good record of sale and additional printing, and that it is now in the 5th printing only 11 months after its start of sale. This is all from the warm support from my readers. I express my sincere gratitude.

I have received many questions, and requests of consultation and advice from my readers. There are wide varieties of questions, such as concerns of health, which are the most frequent ones, work and people relations, family problems, and memorial services for ancestors.

Quite often I am desperately asked to meet by those who have problems saying: "Though I have asked many people from psychics to counselors for advice, no clue has yet been found for resolution. You are the only one I can rely on." Without any others to turn to for advice, they seem to come to me as their last hope.

Also, I am currently touring Japan to participate in lectures as a guest speaker, and relay gods' words. In meeting my audience, I am surprised to learn that they decided to attend the lecture after reading my book. Also, there are some who say,

"Such a good story must be heard," buy a few dozen copies of my book, and recommend to their friends and families. I am very gracious.

I understand many people are going through hard times, and are suffering. I hope to be even the slightest helping hand to those by publishing my books. Thus, I have decided to write my second book.

My mission as a spiritual counselor is to relay gods' words to people living in this world right now, and to help them by guiding them to the right path. The great response to my first book may mean that what I am doing helps even a little.

This book will differ in content from my first work. My experiences from my early childhood were the basis of the 1st volume. This book will pick out and introduce a small portion of the questions I have received, and will introduce gods' precious and deep words in response to them. Gods are sometimes gentle, and are also strict at other times, giving us their messages in hopes for the happiness of those in need. By my speaking those messages on behalf of gods, often worries and concerns are led to a resolution.

I encourage my readers to apply to themselves as you read this book. By comparing gods' words to your own life, and listening to their words, I believe you will be able to find a hint to a resolution.

Recently, healing-spots traveling and appreciation of Buddhist statues have become a trend. It is believed that each Japanese temple or shrine has a healing-spot. The fact that these places have gained attention proves that people are seeking for comfort and peace in this restless society.

This trend is not only triggered by people's seeking tranquility. At the basis of this is their desire for deities, that is, God and gods.

The realm where God and other deities abide is called "the Realm of Deity," and we, human beings, will be able to ascend to that world once we finish our lives in this world 30 times. Deities in the Realm of Deity have faces like those of statues of Buddha, and this is probably why people feel calm when they see these statues. People's souls have started to reach out for deities unconsciously. I believe this is a good sign.

Deities do exist. As a spiritual counselor, I have received messages from God or other deities on "The future of humanity and the earth," "The real purpose to live a life," "The right way to live as a human," "The real structure (the true aspect) of this world and the universe," and so on. I will introduce some parts of these topics, so I hope you will give this book a read.

Table of Contents

Prologue ·· 1

Chapter 1 Miracle Counseling
A flood of counseling requests ··· 10
Cases of schizophrenia ·· 12
   The boy who still had his past life memories ································ 12
Cases of depression ·· 15
   The girl who saw dragon gods ··· 15
   The man attached by animal spirits ·· 18
   The doctor attached by earthbound spirits in the hospital ············· 21
   The causes of panic disorder and hyperventilation syndrome ·············· 29
Cases of those who suffer from intractable diseases ························ 30
   The woman who suddenly developed ALS ································ 30
   The man possessed by tree dragons (natural spirits) ···················· 35
Cases of person with terminal cancer ····································· 39
   The female terminal cancer patient who reflected on her sin of her past life ···· 39
Cases of intrauterine children in a feet-first orientation ······················ 40
   A breech baby is resisting parents ·· 40
   The pregnant woman who reflected on herself, leading her breech baby to the normal position ·· 41
   My own experience of delivery—delivery is the great chance to awake spiritually ·· 44
Cases of those requested to pay a large amount of money by psychics and fortune-tellers ·· 50
   The person requested by a psychic to pay a large amount of money ········ 50
   The couple whose underwear was burnt by a fortune-teller ·················· 51
   The person requested by a psychic to pay a large amount of money for changing the watcher spirit ·· 53
   The person who resold the fabricated investment package to his acquaintances ·· 55
   The woman who escaped from ¥30 million loss ···························· 57

Importance to have a good judgment and recognize the truth 58
Cases of wrong memorial services for ancestors 61
The proper service for ancestors is to offer meals wholeheartedly............ 61
No need to spend much money for family Buddhist alters and graves...... 65
Ancestors who have ascended to gods protect offspring..................... 67
The chances of ancestors' souls being born as pets 70

Chapter 2　Miracle Lectures

My guest appearances at the Miracle Lectures 76
The halls of the lectures are full of spirits... 81
Reasons why the hall is glittering gold 84
Reunion in tears with deceased family members 86
Your attendance at the lectures saves souls....................................... 95
Only one evening meal together with ancestors 97
The toxins of the parts possessed by spirits start to melt 99
Various miracles occurring to the participants of the lectures 104
Cleansing reaction is the sign of recovery... 106
A psychiatrist attends the lectures.. 109
Long queues at the autograph sessions 110
People are reaching out for the lectures 114

Epilogue
The time has come for the Japanese to be awaken to their mission 119

Afterword.. 141

Chapter 1

Miracle Counseling

A flood of counseling requests

I am currently working as a spiritual counselor relaying gods' messages, calling forth and communicating with ancestors, and helping solve the problems of diseases and difficulties of those in need. In this chapter, I would like to share gods' messages in response to those problems.

What I do in the counseling is called "spiritual investigation," which is allowed by gods. Through this spiritual investigation, spirits attached to the bodies and spiritual phenomena can be clarified. Furthermore, by communicating with gods, I can understand not only the disease but also the condition of physical body and the thoughts (only of those allowed by gods).

Many of those who come to consult me have various problems, suffer from serious and rare diseases, and are diagnosed with mental illnesses. Some of them suffer trauma besides diseases, and worry about not being able to change their flaws or improve themselves. Others also worry about unsuccessful business or poor relationship at their workplace and home.

By giving spiritual investigation to them, the causes of serious diseases and unfortunate events becomes clear in many cases. Through counseling, miracles such as recovering from diseases and improving their fortune happen.

Spiritual investigation, however, requires ultimate concentration to channel with beings in other dimensional spaces.

Chapter 1 Miracle Counseling

Thus, the physical and mental burden is too heavy for me to comply with all counseling requests.

After my book was published, however, inquiries from readers for counseling flooded into the publishing firm. As I had informed the publisher of the difficulties of accepting counseling in advance, the publisher seemed to be troubled for response. This situation remains unchanged even now.

Quite a few people are still waiting for their turns. We have a prerequisite that, in order to apply for counseling, a family member or the person himself/herself should have attended one of our lectures that I will mention in the 2nd chapter.

Among those who come to me for counseling, some are diagnosed with mental diseases, depression, or hikikomori (or withdrawal). Their family members are often anxious about whether they can leave for counseling due to the fluctuation of their condition on that day. However, those chosen for counseling by gods are mysteriously able to leave the house.

Many of those who hope to see me request earlier counseling, but I will basically see them in order of application.

However, we have an exception. Quite rarely a god tells me to give counseling earlier to those who could be saved because of their earlier stage in their diseases. Let me add that I am unable to alter the order.

Now we would like to introduce several cases of counseling that could benefit readers. I will omit some personal information, and change the content a little due to protection of their privacy.

Cases of schizophrenia

The boy who still had his past life memories

People diagnosed with schizophrenia increasingly come to see me for counseling. Schizophrenia is one of the mental disorders with symptoms of visual and auditory hallucinations, and delusions. Families of the diagnosed patients worry about and take them to me for counseling.

Recently, a mother came in for counseling with her son who was hospitalized for schizophrenia. I asked her, "Why did you let him be hospitalized?" and she answered, "One day, he suddenly started talking nonsense." He talked about something so unreasonable that his family could hardly understand, so his family was quite at a loss what to do with him until he finally punched his father out of frustration. This event discouraged his family to stay with him, and took him to the hospital. Then a doctor diagnosed him with schizophrenia, and required him 3 months of hospitalization.

While I was listening to his mother, I heard a god say, "His words and behavior have something to do with his past life." So I asked the god in detail about his past life—he was alive in the Edo period. I relayed the details to his family.

Chapter 1 Miracle Counseling

Both the mother and son were astonished with their eyes wide open. "What he was talking before his hospitalization was exactly the same as you mentioned now!" said the mother.

This means that he was trying to tell his family about his memories of his past life. Even though he stayed hospital as a patient of schizophrenia, in fact, his communication ability was just normal. In this case, the mother had attended our lecture and wanted her son to see me, so she obtained permission for temporary leave from the hospital and took his son all the way to Gifu Prefecture.

When the two first arrived, I told her, "There is nothing wrong with your son." The memories of his past life still remained, and he was just speaking about them. I assume that the memories of his past life and those of present life. including the current events might be jumbled up, which caused him to incidentally speak of his memories of his past life. He felt regret and sorry about having given his father a punch, saying: "I know I am to blame for having said mean things and punched my father, but he never tried to understand me. One day I flew into a fit of rage at his word, 'You are insane!' "

Since then, the son continued his story about his memories of his past life. It all exactly matched up what a god told me. For a while we were enjoying a lively conversation over his past life, and his mother was listening to it with her mouth wide open in wonder.

Even though the son was diagnosed with schizophrenia, there was nothing wrong with him. He just still held his past life memories. I explained about it to his mother, asking her to let him out of the hospital so that he could stop taking unnecessary medicine such as tranquilizers which might cause some negative effect on his body.

In this case, it is very important for his family to fully understand the son, besides letting him leave hospital. First of all, his family needs to recognize the fact that he still has his past life memories, accept the situation, and try to deal with him frankly and warmly. Then, the son will surely be able to live his life calmly without feeling neglected.

They were both very pleased with the counseling, and said to me: "We are really glad to meet you. We cannot thank you enough."

Surprisingly the son's look when they left was totally different from that when they came in. The son left with a relaxed and calm expression, saying to me: "I almost lost self-confidence because my family failed to understand me, flatly rejecting what I said. I started thinking myself insane, but now I've recovered my confidence, thanks to you." Learning that he has nothing unusual in his speech and behavior, he was able to regain his nearly lost self-confidence. I felt so happy to see his satisfactory look.

In case of schizophrenia, even doctors sometimes fail to

identify its cause. Because of its unidentified cause, doctors are likely to diagnose the complaint as schizophrenia, making the patients calm and quiet by prescribing tranquilizers. However, even if patients are diagnosed with schizophrenia, in fact, many of them are not the case. Just like this case, its cause could sometimes be from the memories of one's past life, spiritual interference stemming from vengeful spirits of past life, and so on. I am not denying going to see a doctor, but I just hope to let people know that the truth may come out after spiritual investigation. Recently the number of doctors who came to understand this reality has increased. I have been informed that those doctors visit the lectures I participate in as a guest speaker.

Cases of depression

The girl who saw dragon gods

Those who suffer from depression often come to me for counseling. Recently, a mother took her daughter with depression and withdrawal (or hikikomori) to me. The woman had attended the lecture before, and wanted to let her daughter see me.

The mother was worried about her daughter, and said: "She says she sees a snake in the hallway of our house, but no one in our family is able to see it. Could she be insane?"

I conducted spiritual investigation, and then I heard a god say, "This girl sees dragon gods not snakes." Apparently, in the land of their house, dragon gods have abided since a long time ago, and the daughter is able to see their appearances.

Furthermore, the god continued: "The ancestor of them, several generations back, received a message from a god to build a house over that land. So they moved to the waste land, brought the land into cultivation, and built their own house there."

When I relayed this message to the mother, she said: "I heard the story that our ancestors, some generations back, had moved to the current lot all of a sudden and built the house. Since then, over several generations, we have lived there. I was always wondering what made our ancestors suddenly decide to move to such a rural area. But now I can make it out, thanks to you." She looked fully convinced.

Through my clairvoyance, I found that their land was pretty vast and the building which looked like a Shinto shrine was there. I assume dragon gods stay in that building. Thus, it is not that dragon gods live in the family's house, but that they built a house over the land protected by the dragon gods. The daughter, who is particularly sensitive and receptive in a spiritual sense, was able to see the figure of these dragon gods from time to time.

This daughter does not have depression, either. It's simply

that she can see dragon gods. I explained that, and asked her mother to let her family accept and understand what she says.

It doesn't matter how the others may say about her. Above all, her family should understand what she is trying to say. If she says, "I can see a snake," her family members should respond to her accordingly, and say: "Really? Where is it? Then let's say 'thank you' to the snake." Such a warm but simple response will greatly help those who can see the spirits relax and calm down.

Some families are likely to show negative attitude toward those who insist on being able to see spirits, and jump to the conclusion that they must be insane or they must be possessed by evil spirits. If that is the case, family can be the source of the cause of depression. The fact that even the closest family members fail to understand them tends to psychologically drive them into a corner, leading to develop depression.

I received a message from a god for those whose family members are suffering from withdrawal, NEET (not in employment, education, or training), or truancy. I do hope it will be very helpful and instructive to you.

A message from a god

Those who are under the condition of NEET, withdrawal, or truancy are never ever lazy.

*They themselves fully recognize that this situation
should not be acceptable.
People around them need to give more understanding
and support to them.
It is not only just one's own problem.
It is also a problem created by society.
In a sense, this has been triggered by the warped
and strained society
Still young and innocent people with pure soul
are becoming victims.
Even if the society is as it is, by showing them role models
who somehow overcome difficulties and live meaningful lives
with graceful mind,
they are able to go out free from anxiety.
Supporters including family members, friends,
and acquaintances should look for the better environment
which suits them.
Only those who are very close to them are able to help them out.
They are all anxiously waiting for their reaching out
a helping hand.*

The man attached by animal spirits

Next I will introduce you another case of people suffering from depression.

The man was a farmer possessed by a huge number of animal spirits. His elder sister had attended our lecture before, and took him to me out of concern about him.

After a briefing, I did spiritual investigation to find out there were several other causes besides animal spirits. Then I relayed the message from a god to him, but he suspiciously listened to me in a bad temper, leaning back in a chair.

He had every reason for being in a bad mood. He was taken to me almost forcibly by his sister, and was abruptly told that animal spirits attached to him. It is quite understandable that he could not bring himself to believe. He didn't seem to accept that, and said to me, "Could it possibly happen that people are possessed by animal spirits?"

However, his attitude dramatically changed once we started talking about their house. While conducting spiritual investigation, I saw through the house with clairvoyant power, and found many earthbound spirits. Then I located the exact spots of the garage where earthbound spirits were haunting in large numbers. I also explained in detail of their house. The man, who had been sitting back in a chair all the time, suddenly leaned forward and started whispering in his sister's ear in wonder: "Why on earth does this woman know the details of our house? It is as if she was getting a peep at our house." "See, I told you so. She can see even invisible things," his sister quietly responded.

Then I read the man's mind and explained everything to

him. He exclaimed in surprise: "Wow . . . you got me. I can't hide anything from you. You saw through my mind . . . Could this happen actually?"

After counseling was over, he went home while mumbling to himself: "How come could the woman see inside my house and even my mind? How could it be possible?"

In his case, I removed his attaching spirits after giving him an explanation, "From now, I am going to cut and eliminate animal spirits attached to you, and then you will recover from depression." This art of "cutting spirits" is also called "exorcism." I do this only to the attaching spirits which cause troubles, and when gods judge that they would never make a realization. If the spirits belong to ancestors or have still chances to make a realization, they are admonished and guided accordingly.

He might have felt queer to have his attaching spirits cut. I think, however, I was able to make him understand even slightly that invisible world does exist. Later, his health condition has considerably improved, and he has recovered from depression. I was really relieved to hear that.

If those who attended our lectures before come to me for counseling, they have already understood about me to some extent. Those who meet me for the first time, however, tend to get astonished during counseling so much that I sometimes enjoy their reaction in wonder.

Chapter 1 Miracle Counseling

Gods probably try to teach the truth, which cannot be realized otherwise, much more to those who are skeptical of invisible world. Gods wish to save those people. That's why gods teach them the truth that invisible world does exist by giving them experiences of miracle.

My ability is nothing amazing, but gods use my body in order to relay the message: "Deities do exist in this world. We hope that everyone will accept this reality and existence of deities, and will believe what we preach you. This is the best way that you are saved."

The doctor attached by earthbound spirits in the hospital

I have one more case of a person with depression that I would like to share with you.

The man, a doctor, got sick immediately after he started to work at a certain hospital, and was diagnosed with depression.

After talking with him for a while, I conducted a spiritual investigation. I found out too many earthbound spirits in his hospital. The doctor is so generous that those earthbound spirits seemed to attach to him right off the bat to find him. Moreover, his psychological aspect was also one of the causes.

Generally there are quite a few earthbound spirits and wandering spirits in the hospitals, because those who pass away during operations will become earthbound spirits. Also, even after people die of diseases, their pain will last. That is why they wander about the hospital as wandering spirits, hoping that doctors in hospital may relieve their pain.

I received the detailed instructions about the doctor from a god as follows: "He should quit the hospital he is currently working at, and work at that hospital instead"; "He should be the medical specialist in this specific field"; "He might as well depend on this professor." I was surprised at them because it is quite rare for a god to give such specific instructions.

Those who get the instructions can be divided into two groups based on their response: one group is those who obediently follow them, and the other is those who just nod and forget them. Those two groups of people are supposed to follow the quite different paths. Those who obediently accept gods' words and take an action immediately will receive divine arrangements, which means that their lives will be realized just as they hope.

Many of those people later say to me in appreciation: "Thanks to you, my physical condition has improved a lot. Thank you very much." Putting gods' messages into practice brings about the solution to anxieties and diseases.

On the other hand, some people come back to me asking for counseling again. They are less likely to receive divine arrangements. I ask them, "Did you comply with gods' instructions and put them into practice?" Most of them reply, "I tried to do so, but eventually failed." They are not able to get divine

Chapter 1 Miracle Counseling

arrangements because they failed to follow instructions from gods.

Good timing also matters in putting gods' words into practice. For instance, if you act on gods' messages after one year, you will never ever receive divine arrangements. It is too late. You should not lose out on the chance. Upon receiving the words from gods, take an action in a timely manner.

In the event that you fail to follow up on instructions from gods, you might have more troubles. The gods are watching all the course of your behavior. Unless you act up to the instructions, in spite of having accepted it, the gods might try to give you more hardship in order to make you aware of the situation you are in. Gods instruct you only what you can do. It goes without saying that gods never give you any instruction that costs you some money. So please feel relieved.

Most of those who come to see me for counseling seem to seriously follow the instructions. Since they ask for counseling from their heart, they are willing to listen to gods' words.

Diseases and misfortunes are caused not only by spiritual interference but also by problems in their mind. There are some cases where they are given diseases and misfortunes to make them reflect on their conduct and thoughts, reviewing their past. "We would like to awake them from the current state while they are alive"; "We do hope they somehow notice their mission"; Out of gods' tender feeling, they hope to convey the messages to those in need to help them out.

Some of those who come to see me for counseling are not actually interfered by spirits. Their mind causes the problems. In that case, gods quite often tell them what parts of their characters or thoughts need to be improved. Gods occasionally scold them severely in a rage, which is most likely to happen to those with higher social rank or status. Those people may have few chances to reflect themselves since no people around them dare to correct their behavior or give them any advice.

Thus, if you receive instructions from gods, your disease and misfortune will move toward solutions and your life will change for the better by reflecting yourselves and correcting your behavior as instructed.

I received a message from a god as to emotional pain. I hope you would use the following message as a guide of your future.

A message from a god

The reason you become painful in your heart is
that you think only about yourself.
The reason you become worn out in your heart is that
you fail to be considerate for others,
unable to get any feeling of happiness to live for others.
"Why am I surrounded by people so distressed?
Why do they come to me?" you might wonder,

but it is you yourself that draw those people up to you.
You and those people are pretty much alike.
You can easily find your soul level
if only you look people around you.
Your defects in your character,
which should be corrected in order to improve yourself,
can hardly be recognized on your own.
Then observe those around you closely, your family, friends,
and acquaintances.
What parts about them bother you? Do you dislike those parts?
"I hate my husband's insensibility";
"I dislike my parents' being nagging and opinionated";
"I do not like my friend's telling a lie";
"I feel abhorrent to see the sullen looks of man next door";
"I am intolerant of my children's being unpunctual";
"I don't like my grandmother's being unable to catch the mood."
Probably you will come up with more and more complaints.
Those are, however, true of you, too.
All of them are applicable to you.
Since you have just the same qualities in your complaints,
you notice them in others.
Unless you have the same,
you will never notice those negative qualities.
(This does not apply to those who do heinous acts
such as criminals.)

*Using people around you, we are teaching you
what you should change about yourself.
If you notice something disgusting in someone,
first try to reflect on yourself.
Then, you should ask yourself if you have the same disposition,
if so, you should make efforts every day to correct it.
Your continuous efforts accordingly will elevate the level of soul
of those around you.
This is when you enter the further advanced stage.
Their attitude, words, and behavior toward you
will certainly change for the better.
Hearts of your family may be improved.
New friends and new acquaintances will come together
around you.
Then you will recognize that you have advanced
to the next stage.
Life is a place where you are supposed to do life practices.
Therefore, it is a matter of course
that you experience various difficulties.
It is up to you whether you feel painful or enjoyable
for life practices given to you.
Feeling painful, you can hardly go forward.
Feeling enjoyable, you can advance further and further, and
moreover something new and nice would take place.
Your efforts to change your mental attitude*

could improve your future life.
Having said that, you may still think
that you cannot feel happy in your daily life.
Try looking for people around you who are very lively, cheerful,
and energetic with a forward-looking attitude.
Try having friendly relations with them positively,
and your way of thinking will change for the better
little by little before you are aware of it.
This is one of the ways to forcefully bring you up to the next step.
If you find a wonderful role model,
you should make friends with the person,
and completely absorb and adopt his/her excellent points
to yourself by mimicking,
which will improve you eventually, too.
Everyone can do it, as it is by no means difficult.

In addition to reflecting on your daily behavior, I have one more to mention. I would like you not to always attribute your poor physical condition to spiritual interference. As I have explained, in some cases, your disease and misfortune could be caused by problems in your heart.

Conducting spiritual investigations could remove the spirits that cause damage to the body. However, some people still complain of their bad condition even after those spirits are gone. As a reason, it could be from their strong feeling of anxiety about spiritual interference: "I may be possessed by another bad spirit"; "I feel somehow I am possessed by spirits." Those feelings of excessive concern could trigger disease and misfortune.

Change your way of thinking and start afresh after they are removed by spiritual investigations, otherwise you won't be able to make a clean break with your weak constitution forever.

Then, what is required to get out of your long-time weak constitution? It is to hold your own firm axis. You should make efforts to be stronger mentally and physically without ascribing disease and misfortune to all bad spirits.

It is indeed true that, among those to whom spirits are attached, some people are interfered by the spirits very badly but others are not. Its difference results from whether they have their own firm axis or not. Those with their own axis are most unlikely to be manipulated by spirits.

Then, how can we obtain our own axis? First and foremost, think positively with a sense of purpose, and laugh a lot. Your big laugh could even shake off the attaching spirits in a flash. Spirits feel really uncomfortable to be with people who are cheerful, and smiling all the time with positive thinking.

On the other hand, spirits like to be with worriers and whiny people. Those who are easily depressed tend to think negatively, have frequent emotional ups and downs, and are more likely to be attached by spirits. As a result, people without

Chapter 1 Miracle Counseling

their own axis are probably more susceptible to troubles of spirits.

The causes of panic disorder and hyperventilation syndrome

There are cases where panic disorder and hyperventilation syndrome are triggered by possession of spirits. In this case, however, the cause is not a vengeful spirit grudging to that person but the spirit which happens to attach to the person hoping to depend on them. Thus, they will never ever get involved in such a worst case as to life-threatening situations.

When you suffer from a seizure, I suggest that you should see yourself objectively in a seizure, regarding your pain as that of spirits, saying, "It must be very hard and painful for you, spirits." And then, the seizure could soon disappear after the spirits make full realization. Those who suffer from panic disorder and hyperventilation syndrome are, in a sense, excellent people because they are likely to be relied on by others, according to a god.

With their own axis, those who suffer could feel better, fixing the center of them. I suggest that they should apply themselves to this way.

You do not have to worry even if some spirits are attached to you. If you live cheerfully with positive thinking based on your firm axis, you will never be manipulated by them.

Cases of those who suffer from intractable diseases

The woman who suddenly developed ALS

People suffering from intractable diseases often come to see me for counseling.

A female in her mid-20s with her back making a 90-degree turn, like an aged woman, came to see me.

When she came at first time, a god let me not conduct any spiritual investigation. Instead, the god mentioned: "Go to this hospital first. Probably ALS (amyotrophic lateral sclerosis) will be suspected. If so, come here again."

Following the advice, the woman visited the hospital and later came back to me, saying: "As you told, I was diagnosed with ALS. It is said to be one of the intractable diseases characterized by muscle atrophy and progressive weakness. There is no known cause for this disease, or no medical treatment has been available yet. The doctor is not sure whether there is any possibility of my recovery. I have no idea what I should do."

Looking at her appearance, I found her back bent at right angles, her body leaning over with her mouth watering and even with a difficulty in speaking. She had not had any problem until she became 20. She got married, gave birth a baby, and, after a while, she suddenly developed ALS.

Her family members, including her husband, and even her neighbors came in her company. Since they once attended our lecture, they decided to take her to me out of concern.

I usually conduct spiritual investigation at the exclusive room. But, in this case, before I led them into that room, I had no choice but to start to read the spirit. Her attached spirits jumped out of her body, and then took possession of those who were around her.

When I conduct spiritual investigation in the usual manner, I have some staff who are possessed easily assist, and let the spirits enter them. In this case, however, the spirits which had originally been attached to the woman could not help waiting and jumping out of her body, and took possession into the bodies of about 20 people around her. Those attaching spirits manifested on their bodies. This is a phenomenon that people's bodies are manipulated by spirits. They tend to sway and scream because they can feel the spirits' emotion and agony as well. All about 20 people possessed with these spirits started to scream all at once as if they had been quite different people: "I was killed at that time. I can hardly breathe!"

A god told me that vengeful spirits were attached to the woman as she had been obliged to kill a great number of people by burying them alive in her past life. It was the order of her boss. Therefore, she had no choice but to follow it as it was her past job. (Let me omit the explanation of the motives of the crime and the human relationships behind it.) However, victims usually have a grudge against not a person who ordered but a person who buried them alive at first hand. Even though she had been ordered by her boss in her past life, in this present life, she was interfered by those many spirits whose lives had been put an end by her hand.

When the spirits were detached after spiritual investigation, all people manipulated by spirits looked bewildered, saying, "Did I scream something strange?" Actually they do not have to worry about anything. They were only temporarily manipulated by spirits. Even in the case that spirits manifest on their bodies, they will return to normal soon after the spirits leave their bodies.

In this way, an unexpectedly open spiritual investigation was performed, and the details of the sin in her past life were relayed to her. Then, I told her that she would recover from her illness only if she starts to reflect seriously on her past conduct. In her case, it was only a short while after she developed the disease; therefore, her physical damage was not so severe that there was good prospect of complete recovery.

I relayed the message from a god, and she and her family reflected on their conduct from the bottom of their hearts in tears. Then, a miracle happened. After the spiritual investigation was over, past vengeful spirits made a full realization, and thereby they left her body. Simultaneously the woman's back, which had been bent at right angles, was straightened up! People around her were just astonished to see her dramatic sud-

Chapter 1 Miracle Counseling

den change. Thereafter she made a surprisingly quick recovery, and got well again about one month after the spiritual investigation.

Later she came to thank me for her recovery. I was surprised to see her appearance, because she looked so much younger than before. On second thoughts, since she was in her mid-20s, it makes sense that she looked young. When I met her first time, she looked like an aged woman with her back bent greatly. Therefore, she must have looked quite a different woman as she returned to herself, an ordinary young woman at her age.

Let me add one more to her case. In addition to the past vengeful spirits, she was interfered by the spirit of an aged woman. The spirit seems to have attached herself to that young woman when she paid a visit to the local shrine with her family to cerebrate the 7-5-3 day (a Shinto ritual to pray for the healthy growth of children of three, five, and seven years of age). During the spiritual investigation, I also removed the spirit of this aged woman.

Such intractable diseases as her case usually appear when they are born, or after they become adult all of a sudden. A god says, "People are more likely to develop these diseases while they are enjoying happy life, such as when they become college students, or adolescent boys or girls, when they get married, or after giving birth."

After people die and leave this world, they have to purify all their sins in their past lives, and then they are reincarnated. However, vengeful spirits which failed to depart in peace due to grudges against those people are wandering this world, patiently waiting for their reincarnation for hundreds of years, "I'll take revenge on them." Vengeful spirits are so scary.

In the spiritual investigation, I sometimes explain about the past sins committed by those who come to see me for counseling. I always encourage them by saying, "You don't have to feel any responsibility for your past sins, and there is no need to blame yourself." Even if they committed sins in their past lives, they have already worked so hard to atone for their past sins in the Astral Realm, rising to the Spirit Realm, from which they are reincarnated into this world. Thus, their poor health condition and misfortune are not caused by their past sins but vengeful spirits.

One of the major roles of spiritual investigation is to remove the attaching vengeful spirits. Those vengeful spirits themselves are also suffering since they have kept holding grudges for hundreds of years. Removing, and saving, the vengeful spirits will result in saving the people who are interfered by them.

During the spiritual investigation, gods admonish vengeful spirits with words filled with deep mercy. My body being used during that, I can feel gods' affection so profound that I often find it quite difficult to hold my tears. I wonder if human beings can do the same . . . I'm afraid not.

Chapter 1 Miracle Counseling

The man possessed by tree dragons (natural spirits)

Let me show you another case with ALS.

When I was asked for spiritual investigation by the family of a person with ALS, years had already passed since he developed the disease. He was bedridden, unable to move any muscle except that of his face. His family, who had attended our lecture, applied for my spiritual investigation.

As he was bedridden, spiritual investigation was conducted through videophone. Then, a god said, "Vengeful spirits in his past life and also tree dragons, which caused his disease, are attached to him." Some tree dragons, which are natural spirits, dwell in particular old trees. A tree dragon, which is in grey and a few meters tall, has a quite different soul itself from that of dragon gods in the Realm of Deity. The man cut down the tree in which tree dragons had dwelt, which provoked the tree dragons, and they attached themselves to him.

I explained to him all about the attaching tree dragons, and told him to seriously reflect on having cut down the tree. Through the videophone, I urged the attaching tree dragons to leave, and then the man reflected on his past conduct deeply in tears. As some spirits besides tree dragons had been attached to his body, in the same way I guided them to leave him.

In his case, the disease had already reached an advanced stage, and a god said that a complete recovery could hardly be expected. A week after the spiritual investigation, however, he was able to move his legs and grasp one's hand. His doctor was so surprised even with his small changes because he had not been able to move his limb only an inch before.

Thus cutting down the trees where tree dragons dwell might cause misfortune. If you unavoidably have to cut down the tree, first of all, you need to explain about the situation to the tree dragons carefully and thoughtfully so that they can fully understand and accept it. You can talk to them in our language. You should start to explain the situation to them at least one month before you plan to cut down the tree: "Such being the case, I am afraid I have to cut down the tree. Would you mind moving to another tree?"

In the case of a big tree, it would be much nicer if you informed the tree of pruning, saying, "Let me trim the branches of the tree from now." If your advance explanation to the tree dragons is sufficient enough to convince them, they will unlikely hold grudges against you.

Unfortunately some people die because of tree dragons' curse. There used to be a big, old tree near my house. Children used to enjoy climbing it. The tree, however, was cut down by the landowner for leveling of ground.

I was so surprised and scared to see the felled trees that I couldn't help saying to the children: "The tree that tree dragons had dwelt in was cut down. Something awful may happen to the master of the house." Though I prayed that it would not

Chapter 1 Miracle Counseling

take place, the anger of the tree dragons against the master didn't subside; thus he suddenly passed away within a year.

According to his family, while he was sitting on the sofa, his heart suddenly stopped, and later he was found dead. It was when he was in his mid-50s, in the prime of life. I was not acquainted with him, but I should have mustered up the courage to say, "Tree dragons are angry with you." It did not matter if he might have thought me insane. I still regret not having warned him.

The anger of tree dragons is likely to be directed at a house owner. If the house is newly built or enlarged on the ground with earthbound spirits, or the house with earthbound spirits is demolished, the brunt of the spirits' anger is also directed at a house owner in most cases. Therefore, I recommend you should collect earthbound spirits first if you plan to put up a new house, or extend, or remodel, a building (see pp. 71–74).

In the same manner as in trees, when you cut off a flower or trim a foliage plant, I suggest you should prune them while apologizing, "I am sorry but let me trim this part." Plants never hold grudges against people, but of course they have their own lives. They seem to feel a kind of pain when they are cut down and trimmed. So I hope you take a great care of plants, remembering that they also have lives.

I received a message from a god for people with intractable diseases and congenital defects as follows:

A message from a god

Some people were born with brain damage.
They grow a little slowly, and are mentally retarded.
These are only the problems of their physical bodies,
but their souls are sound.
In communicating, people understand its content in their brain,
and simultaneously they can listen and understand in their soul,
as well.
Therefore, do not talk in infants' language
to those with brain defects and dementia,
or, do not ignore, or exclude, them from a loop of conversation,
thinking: "I am afraid they are not able to understand";
"Their response is too slow to continue conversation."
They properly listen to, and understand, all,
which leads to their own soul's sound growth.
This is true of people in a vegetative state.
Actually talking to them may be a one-way conversation,
however, they respond to you in their heart
by listening to your conversation in their soul and heart.
They are able to listen to stories, rejoice in their heart, grieve,
get angry, and cry . . . with emotions.
This is also applicable to babies and infants who can't talk well.
Keep in mind that human's soul and heart are able to recognize

*and understand everything
no matter how their physical condition may be.
Do not be rude to them. Be always nice and polite to them.*

Cases of person with terminal cancer

The female terminal cancer patient who reflected on her sin of her past life

A female terminal cancer patient given only a month to live asked me for spiritual investigation. She strongly wished to know about sins of her past life and the cause of her cancer before she would leave this world.

At that time, she was already bedridden in the hospital. Therefore, I performed spiritual investigation through videophone again in the same way as in the case I mentioned before. However, we had a difficulty in adjusting the schedule to fix the date. Even though it was March when she was told the rest of her life, I eventually conducted the spiritual investigation in autumn of the year. She was said to have been struggling to live her life saying: "I can't end my life now. I have to live until I take spiritual investigation." She spent days looking forward to it.

At last the schedule adjustments worked out, and I conducted spiritual investigation to find that she seriously reflected on herself. Only a week after that, she passed away peacefully in her sleep. Her terminal cancer gnawed away at the body; however, she died a gentle and easy death without any pain.

Later her daughter came to see me. Together with the daughter, the spirit of the deceased female appeared. Turning her face toward me, the deceased female thanked me with her hands putting together: "I was really looking forward to having my spirit read by you. After the spiritual reading, I felt much better. Thank you very much." She learned her sins by spiritual investigation and showed genuine regret, reflecting on herself wholeheartedly until she died. This must have saved her soul. The facial expression of the female spirit was very cheerful, changing dramatically from the one in agony when she was struggling with her cancer. I was relieved to see her calm and satisfied look.

This event made me realize again that my mission is to ascend people's souls, though it is impossible as to their physical bodies, to the better place.

Cases of intrauterine children in a feet-first orientation

A breech baby is resisting parents

Pregnant women, worrying about their babies in breech position, often come to see me for counseling. In the case that baby's position changes to breech position when the due date draws near in the last month of pregnancy, it is said to be quite difficult to return its position to normal. That's why they have strong feelings of anxiety.

In this case, I do not ask gods but babies for the reason of their breech position, because it is the babies that know the reason best.

Breech position is likely to be caused by baby's resistance against their parents. By resisting themselves in the belly, babies try to make their dad or mam realize their faults that should be corrected. Thus, if their parents notice the messages from their unborn babies and look back on their daily behavior, reflecting on themselves accordingly, the breech position will return to the normal position, leading them to wonderful childbirth.

Taking this into account, I think breech baby is not always a negative factor, since it teaches parents' faults to be corrected. There are many who suffer from hard labors without any chance of realization due to lack of such symptom. If some of you happen to be uneasy about your breech baby, review your everyday conduct, saying to yourself, "My baby is trying to give me a wake-up call."

The pregnant woman who reflected on herself, leading her breech baby to the normal position

Not a few women easily got their breech babies turn head-down after counseling.

One of them came to see me a few days before the expected date of birth. Her doctor said to her: "As your baby is breech, you will have a C-section. You should go into hospital tomorrow."

After briefing with her about her baby, I asked her baby about the reason of her being breech. Then the baby gave me several answers.

The first one is that the baby wanted the woman to stop nagging her husband. He is a car enthusiast, buying car parts for converting within the budget of his means. The woman seems to have been complaining about that. "My mam is always grumbling about my dad. However hard she objects to him buying that stuff, he will never listen to her and continue to buy it because he loves cars. If she can't stop him anyway, let him enjoy his favorite pastime to his content," the baby said to me, "My dad is smart enough to stop buying car stuff if his money is running short." The baby talked to me in a mature manner.

The second one is that the baby wanted the woman to take more care of her husband's parents. "My mam always talks with her mam. She seldom talks with her mother in law. They are both my dear grandmothers, so I want my mam to treat them equally."

The baby chatted on various matters for a long time, some of which I could not help laughing to hear. I relayed the two

Chapter 1 Miracle Counseling

messages mainly among them to the woman, saying, "Follow the messages, putting them into action, and seriously reflect on your past conduct, and then your breech will turn to the normal position."

The messages seemed inspiring and moving to her as they were from her own baby in her belly. That night, she wasted no time in apologizing to her husband, and made up her mind to be more attentive to her mother in law. The following day, I received a word filled with joy from her: "This morning I visited a hospital to find that my breech baby turned head-down as you mentioned. Thank you so much." Taking her baby's messages seriously, she looked back on the past, and tried very hard to correct her behavior, which resulted in her baby turning from head-up to head-down.

Not only a breech baby but also the symptoms of placenta previa, for instance, sometimes suggest matters in need of review. Placenta previa, in brief, is an obstetric complication in which the placenta is attached to the uterine wall near the cervix and covers it. Placenta previa can cause massive bleeding during delivery as one of the symptoms. Placenta should be near the top of your uterus and comes out of the birth canal after delivery.

Another woman, with the condition of placenta previa, visited me for counseling. A god instructed her in detail to correct her personality, and she obediently followed the advice and put it into practice. She eventually avoided a C-section and easily gave birth to a baby without heavy hemorrhage.

In this way, childbirth can be a great opportunity to think back to your past and review your conduct.

If a pregnant woman should think: "My life may become hectic after my baby is born"; "Becoming a mother is too early for me," her baby may wind up the umbilical cord around the neck out of concern that the baby itself may cause some trouble to its mother if it is born. The baby twists the cord around the neck as if the baby were trying to commit a suicide. I was surprised to know the profound bond between mother and baby.

My own experience of delivery—delivery is the great chance to awake spiritually

Pregnancy is when a woman comes to her spiritual awakening, according to a god. Since a mother is connected to her baby, sharing time within the mother's body, they are able to use telepathy.

If any expecting mother is reading this, please talk to your baby as much as possible. Also, imagine how the baby would respond to you. As you repeat this, you will notice yourself being able to understand what your baby is thinking. Some may notice to hear the baby's voice itself, while others may feel the baby kick as a response to the mother.

As you continue to communicate with your baby telepathi-

Chapter 1 Miracle Counseling

cally, a safe delivery may be expected. Until the last minute of labor, keep asking your baby: "How are you? Is it almost the time you want to come out?" By coming to her spiritual awakening, the mother as well as the baby is able to go through the delivery calmly while keeping telepathic connections. Then, even after the childbirth, the mother and child will be able to understand each other very well.

In this connection, I would like to share my own episode on childbirth with you.

I gave birth to my first child, a baby girl, at the hospital. Immediately after I gave birth, I was transferred to a private room, where I saw a spirit of a woman who had passed away from uterine cancer. I ended up making the spirit realize and be guided the whole night.

On the night I gave birth to my daughter, somebody suddenly sat on my foot with a thump while I was asleep. Surprised, I woke up to find a spirit of a woman in her 40s there. She said to me: "You are lucky. You are blessed to give birth to a child. I'm here in this form because of an illness in my uterus." I asked her if it was uterine cancer, and she sadly replied yes, looking down. I felt pity for the woman, and attentively listened to her stories.

Since then, while I was at the hospital, the woman spirit visited me every night, and I listened to what she talked, which deprived me of my sleep after childbirth. However, by the time I left the hospital, the spirit seemed to have a full realization and waved goodbye, thanking me.

Although I delivered my first child at a general hospital, a god told me that child delivery is not an illness. So I decided to have the second child in a natural way.

When I became pregnant again, I started to have dreams of myself delivering the baby in my living room. From experience, seeing the same dream multiple times meant that the dream was going to become true. Determined that this was going to happen in real life, I decided to give birth at my home.

There is another reason I chose childbirth at home. I also wanted my 2-year-old daughter to watch her younger brother being born. I wanted them to get along well; so I wanted her to witness the moment of his birth.

If I give birth at the hospital, she might think, "When my mother gets back, she will be holding my rival in her hands." Moreover, she might think, "My mother only cares about the baby, and she doesn't care about me at all," and might get jealous or show regression to baby. By showing her the birth of her younger brother, she might feel the sense of becoming the older sister.

Still, childbirth at home involves its risks. I asked many maternity nurses to help me, but they turned down my offer in the same way, saying, "I cannot take any responsibility." Yet in

Chapter 1 Miracle Counseling

my dreams, a maternity nurse in her 40s helped me. Having the same dream, I told myself I would find this woman, and waited with faith.

Looking forward to seeing the maternity nurse in the dream for a few months, I was near my time of childbirth. Unable to find her, I thought that I had no choice but to go through this alone. Then I started to study seriously how and when I should cut the umbilical cord, how to dispose the placenta, and other things that I should know about delivery in time of need. Getting a set of things necessary for delivery such as scissors, absorbent cotton, and gauze, I made all sorts of preparations.

One day, a friend of mine at a meditation class called me: "I remember you were looking for a maternity nurse. I found that my neighbor is a maternity nurse who specializes in home childbirth. You should meet her." I finally met her, already in my last month of pregnancy with the big belly, and, to my surprise, I found her exactly the same woman I had met in my dream. I knew it had to be her, and I asked her to help me with my delivery. I was thankful to God for bringing me to her.

When the labor pains began at home, I was getting ready to welcome my baby while having a chat with him in my belly. As I have mentioned before, I kept on telepathic communication.

The maternity nurse was also there, awaiting the arrival of my baby. However, around midnight, the baby said to me, "I'm getting so tired that I'm going to take a nap." I was also quite exhausted after finishing lots of things to do before delivery. I said to the nurse, "As my baby said that he is taking a nap, I am going to doze, too"; and fell into a sleep.

Then at around 2 in the morning, the baby woke up and started to move around in my belly again. He told me that it was almost time to go. "My baby said that it is about time for him to come." I said to the nurse. We started our last preparation for the delivery such as boiling water and choosing where I should give birth to him.

To show the moment of childbirth, I woke my 2-year-old daughter. Since she would not stop crying, which is natural considering the time, I ended up holding her, keeping my knees up and leaning onto a chair nearby. And eventually I gave birth to a baby boy past 3 a.m.

Then, to my surprise, the moment the baby was born, she stopped crying, and screamed, "The baby came out!" with her eyes glittering. From her crying face, her facial expression changed into that of an elder sister. And then she stuck with the baby, and kept stroking his head even with the umbilical cord still connected.

As of now, perhaps as a result of showing my daughter her brother's birth, they have a very close relationship, and have not yet fought even once, though my son says it's all thanks to his tolerance . . .

Just recently, I brought home different types of cake for my

Chapter 1 Miracle Counseling

children. My children and I all sat at the table, and I asked which cake they would like. But they would ask each other, "Which one would you like, sister?" "You too, which one would you like?" and we could just not choose. Even now grown up, they are still very close bonded by their mutual concessions.

As I was told by a god that pregnancy is not an illness, my delivery was very easy. Some may doubt this, but I did not feel any pain. I was just carrying my daughter, and, while talking to her, I gave birth to my son very smoothly.

A god said: "Thinking that delivery hurts, it will hurt. Thinking it doesn't hurt, it will not hurt. Whichever to choose is up to you." I chose "no pain," and I also asked the baby hundreds of times to come out without giving me any pain. Even once labor started, I just kept on thinking, "This feels good," instead of "This feels painful," and it actually didn't hurt, rather comfortable. It was a very strange experience. That's when I realized, "Just by changing one's consciousness, people can do anything."

This experience was actually useful in others later too. For example, I had an experience at the dentist as follows. I have heard before that the mother–child relationship used to be much stronger since they breastfed as long as the babies wanted. Following the practice in those days, I gave the breast for an extended period of time until my children themselves refused it. Therefore, when I took dental treatments, I did not want to get anesthesia for fear of bad effects to them. When I had a cavity, I had my tooth pulled out without anesthesia, but I barely felt any pain. The dentist said in surprise, "How could you stand such an intolerable pain without anesthesia?" Similar to the time of the delivery, I chose "no pain," and I told myself that I would never feel any pain.

I shared my own experiences with you, but I am not suggesting, or recommending, childbirth at home. This is just my own episode, and I hope that you would take this just as it is.

Cases of those requested to pay a large amount of money by psychics and fortune-tellers

The person requested by a psychic to pay a large amount of money

Among those who come to visit me, there are many who have been charged large amounts of money by a psychic or a fortune-teller, and ask me if it is something that actually does cost that much.

Thus I would like to introduce you some solutions to those problems, while pointing out some examples.

Here is one consultation example.

After getting counseling from a spiritual medium once, a woman received a phone call asking to leave a few hundred thousand yen in cash at a parking lot. She questioned, "Why should I pay, even after paying the counseling fee?" But the spiritual medium responded with a threat, "If you do not pay, then bad luck will come upon you."

She showed me a picture of the medium. I could tell by the picture that a white fox had possessed the medium. I said to her: "This medium is only threatening you for money; so there is no need for you to pay. In fact, having a relationship with this person is dangerous; so please stop all contact. Don't answer her calls." Since then, she stopped keeping contact with the medium, and the calls never came.

The couple whose underwear was burnt by a fortune-teller

There was also an incident which a fortune-teller burned a couple's undergarments and made the couple pay 200,000 yen. As the husband's business was unsuccessful and, what was worse, the husband became ill, the couple decided to visit the fortune-teller, who charged them a large amount of money.

According to the couple, the first divination session was 50,000 yen an hour, and was told to bring the husband's underwear. They were told that it could be anything worn daily. However, having your underwear seen by another is quite embarrassing. So the wife put on airs a little, and brought his underwear that cost a few ten thousand yen. Then the fortune-teller burned it on the spot, saying that she was going to drive away the misfortune.

Little had they expected that his underwear was burnt, and they were so surprised. However, they could only believe fortune-teller's words, watching it without saying anything. But, that was not the only surprise. The fortune-teller requested them to pay 200,000 yen for the vanishing of the misfortune by burning the husband's underwear. I think the fee for the first session, 50,000 yen, is high enough, though . . .

Since the couple never thought of being demanded for such large amounts of fees, they did not have much cash in hand. The fortune-teller said that there was an ATM at the nearby station so that they could take out some money there, as if it was a fixed routine for her to explain to her clients at every session. The couple could not refuse, and ended up paying the whole amount.

I was asked if this story seemed suspicious, and I replied: "Yes, of course, definitely doubtful. From now, please do not go to that fortune-teller." Furthermore, visiting those types of psychic or fortune-teller, there is a possibility that a bad spirit might actually possess you. This is why it is essential to be able to identify such types.

Even after paying 200,000 yen, the husband's business did not improve, or his health did not take a turn for the better. Then, I did a spiritual investigation, and noticed that their house had many earthbound spirits. So I decided to go to their

Chapter 1 Miracle Counseling

house and pick them up myself. By the next day, the husband's health improved, and even his personality and actions changed for the better, which eventually influenced his business positively. They were very surprised at the outcome. By understanding the roots of the problems, and accurately dealing with them, things do get better.

The person requested by a psychic to pay a large amount of money for changing the watcher spirit

A woman, who was told by a spiritual medium to change the watcher spirit, came to see me. She was cheated out of over 10 million yen.

Consulting the medium for her brother's misfortune, she was told that her brother's watcher spirit was evil, and that, by changing the watcher spirit, his life would change for the better. The medium explained that the fee depended on the levels of the watcher spirit, saying, "For this level of the watcher spirit, it costs 1 million yen; for that level, 5 million . . ."

By the time the woman visited me, she had already paid over 10 million yen. I told her that this was surely a fraud. Even after the watcher spirit was changed, obviously her brother's luck did not improve; on the contrary, he ended up suffering more misfortunes.

I would like to clarify this point. It is impossible to change the watcher spirit by a human. We humans generally have five watcher spirits. They are usually the spirits of ancestors who are in the Spirit Realm, chosen only by a god. This is why humans cannot choose the watcher spirits, nor can we change them later.

However, there are some exceptions. First, when one gets married and the surname changes, so do the watcher spirits. (This is usually happens when one registers one's name into the family register.) For example, when the wife moves into her husband's home, her watcher spirits change to her husband's family's watcher spirits. On the other hand, when the husband moves into his wife's family, his watcher spirits will change to his wife's family's. Once the watcher spirits change, it might happen that his or her personality and their looks change accordingly.

Another exception would be this: when one works hard in his or her lifetime, advancing to the higher levels of soul, a god may change the watcher spirits. The watcher spirits will be replaced to be fitted to the level of the soul of the human, which will make it easier for that person to elevate his/her soul to the next level.

Those who had their watcher spirits replaced may also experience better changes in their physiognomy and their luck. This is only due to God's acknowledgment of your strenuous efforts.

Thus, watcher spirits can't be replaced by humans. I hope you will never be swindled into paying an exorbitant fee.

Chapter 1 Miracle Counseling

There are many others who have visited me for advice on fortune-tellers, psychics, and cults asking for large amounts of money. For example, upon seeking advice from a famous fortune-teller, who frequently appeared on TV, the person was asked for 200,000 yen for a 10-minute session, and was advised to spend a several million yen on a Buddhist altar and a tomb for memorial services for their ancestors. Also, a famous spiritual medium and prolific writer asked a woman for 20,000 yen for only a 2-minute session, all for one word from a god relayed to her, "Hang in there!"

For such an advice which is so simple that anyone can come up with quickly, I think it would be much better to ask your family or friends first than to pay on such an unreasonable demand. If you hesitate to talk to your family, you can invite your friends to dinner, and ask them for advice, for instance. That way, you will be able to have a deeper and thorough feedback from someone who cares you sincerely.

The person who resold the fabricated investment package to his acquaintances

Not only do I get questions about spiritual fraud, but also about investment fraud I am asked for advice.

Recently, a man brought me a letter to one of our lectures, inquiring about an investment fraud he got involved in.

According to the letter, he had been induced to invest in a

fictitious product. In addition, he had sold the product, accidentally tricking some people. Regretting having sold the product and caused trouble to those who bought it, he feared that he might be arrested once the source is found. Later when I performed a spiritual investigation on him, a god said, "The product is surely a fraud; so the money invested in that will not come back."

The man himself had been deceived; thus he had no idea, when selling the product to others, that he was committing a fraud. However, there must have been some monetary attachment or expectations of some profit by introducing this product to others. "He must reflect deeply on his actions, and show sincerity to those who bought the product," said the god.

The man had sold his product to elderly people on their pensions. The god directed that the man should visit these elderly at least once a week instead of hiding away, and said, "If his attitude toward the elderly is sincere enough, the elderly will not sue the man, even if the impostor is arrested." The god added: "By saving others in different ways, he will be saved. He will escape from being sued by being around the lonely elderly, caring, loving, and extending a helping hand to them."

That man is still faithful to the god's guidance, visiting the elderly periodically. He also invites those he wants to save, to our lectures. By following the god's instructions and reflecting on himself, he is living a quiet life without being sued now.

Chapter 1 Miracle Counseling

The woman who escaped from ¥30 million loss

Let me show you another case.

A woman who visited me for counseling had paid over 100 million yen to a fictitious investment deal. A female president of a company in a local area, who was praised on TV as a woman so close to deities as if she was a shrine maiden, had introduced the deal to the woman.

She trusted the female president because of her fame, paying large amounts of money. However, since the interest was not provided, she started to feel suspicious and came to me for advice. Upon questioning the president, she was told that the payment of the interest promised was delayed due to illness of the president, but if she added another 30 million yen, there will be a much greater return. The woman asked me if this was credible.

Once I asked a god, he said: "The female president was an imposter, lying about her illness and trying to evade paying her clients. The woman must stop investing, for she has been deceived. The money spent will not be returned." I relayed the god's words to the woman. However, she tilted her head in confusion, saying, "I don't think she is the woman who could do something like that . . ." She seemed to trust the president almost completely. I was worried that the woman might be swindled again into investing more; so I told her repeatedly to stop investing once and for all as the god instructed her. Later, it was reported on the news that the female president had been arrested on suspicion of fraud. The money she invested, 100 million yen, will never be returned, but I think she was glad that she escaped from being swindled another 30 million yen for the additional investment.

Importance to have a good judgment and recognize the truth

I have met many people troubled by fraud cases. That is especially why I have something to share with you. Above all, I want you to have a good judgment for fortune-tellers, spiritual counselors, even cults, and recognize the truth.

First, upon investment, there is no way that money will be handed to you so easily. I urge those who get involved in conflicts related to money, to ask themselves if they have any attachments to money, thinking: "One way or another, I want to increase these savings," or "I want to increase my pension and my retirement grant by investing." For all their enough money to live a normal, satisfying life, giving in to desires and wanting a more extravagant lifestyle or an easier lifestyle, could end up losing their money.

"It is not good to have too much money," a god continues, "As long as money is being circulated, and there is enough for your daily life, there is no need for you to have more than necessary. Otherwise, the money itself may become the source of troubles and frictions." As a result of leaving too much money

Chapter 1 Miracle Counseling

to children, they may have a quarrel over an inheritance, ending up in a lawsuit. Having too much money can be a negative factor. It is indeed true that money is necessary, but it could be an evil power.

Then, what is important in ascertaining the true fortune-teller and spiritual counselor?

First of all, it is essential to talk to your family and friends, "I am thinking about going to a counselor as such for advice, but what do you think?" I am sure they will answer sincerely.

Recently, a woman came to me for counseling, saying: "My grandmother is a devoted follower of a cult, and she seems to be buying some expensive items from the cult, and applied for a loan. How can I persuade her into leaving the cult?" I told her to bring her grandmother to one of our lectures, and she did.

But the grandmother did not change her mind after the lecture, asserting, "The teaching of my cult is the best." However, like the name of our lectures that is called "Miracle Lectures", there happened a miracle. She had a quarrel with one of the members of the cult, and decided to quit. The family was very glad, and thanked me. It may be one of the good examples in that a victim was saved by a helping hand of his/her family.

In this case, a spirit of a snake attached itself to the grandmother when she became a member of the cult—this cult had a snake spirit. When joining this religious group, snake spirits attach themselves to new members, and as snakes attract, and invite, other snakes, the cult group is being enlarged. By attending one of our lectures, she had her snake spirit eliminated. This is why she could not fit in with the other members anymore and had a fight.

It is ridiculous that you should ask for an approval of the group when you want to quit, and in some cases you should meet conflict on leaving. Leaving a religious group is a fundamental human right, personal freedom. Deities will never oppress, or force, something. Religion is one's desire of deities, and there are no bindings. A religious group, made up out of human's idea without any teachings or even presence of deities, is likely to have many compulsions, management, and bindings.

If it is still necessary to visit a spiritual counselor or a fortune-teller, never fail to check the fee prior to the visit. If, at that point, you are told for example 100,000 yen per hour, it is best to be doubtful. Also it is highly suspicious if they hesitate to tell you the fee before the counseling, make you buy products, or only give you vague answers. If you are unsure, ask someone you can trust for advice, or ask him/her to come with you to the counseling. Always ask for the fee prior to the counseling. With these in mind, you will be able to determine if they are really professional or just frauds.

Chapter 1 Miracle Counseling

Cases of wrong memorial services for ancestors

The proper service for ancestors is to offer meals wholeheartedly

I notice that there are many deceived about memorial services for ancestors. The most frequent question I get asked is, "I was told to pay large amounts of money to fortune-tellers and psychics for advice on giving a service to my ancestors (or earthbound spirits) for the repose of their souls; but is that a relative amount to pay?"

I would like to explain about the proper service for your ancestors.

To begin with the conclusion, there is no need to spend money for the service. What your ancestors hope you to do is to offer dishes wholehartedly, not to ask others to pray for them spending a lot of money.

On the 49th day after death, we will receive a divine judgment, and then our path will be finally decided. Most people are supposed to go to the Astral Realm (four-dimensional space), and atone for the crimes committed in this life.

However, there is no food in the Astral Realm. Though some may wonder if we no longer need to eat when we die, our senses will still remain. Therefore, we will feel hungry without physical bodies. Under such a harsh situation where ancestors have to suffer terrible hunger, they patiently withstand the disciplines.

The type of disciplines depends on the person. For example, the "Snake Hell" is where the jealous and the vengeful go, the most severe "Frozen Hell" is where those with bad personalities and those who committed suicide go, the "Beast Hell" is where those who kept mistresses and those who worked as a spy go, the "Realm of Hungry Ghosts" is where those who caused trouble to others or did not obey the rules of this world go. Whichever hell they are cast into, grueling discipline awaits them. You may be surprised, but just smoking cigarettes would have you end up in hell. As smoking could cause harm to those around you, it is regarded as an action that causes trouble to others greatly. Therefore, those smokers are made to reflect themselves in the afterlife.

In this way, our ancestors under the discipline in the Astral Realm cannot eat. However, once a day, for 25 minutes (only if called by a descendant), they are allowed to go to the descendant for a meal. By offering some warm food in a family altar, our ancestors are able to satisfy their hunger.

The food to be placed in the altar could be the same as that eaten by the family, as long as it is steaming. Then, the ancestors will come to the altar, and, through the golden letters inscribed in the black-lacquered memorial tablet, they are able to extract the steam, satisfying their hunger.

If possible, the golden letters should not be engraved, but

Chapter 1 Miracle Counseling

just be written on the memorial tablet. This is because I would like you to regard the tablet as our human bodies. A god says, "Engraving the memorial tablet would cause the decedents to get hurt or have to get surgery."

There are many ancestors in the altar; so it would be good to offer juice or milk sometimes. If they liked a drink, it would be a good idea to place a beer or hot sake, and enjoy drinking with them saying, "Let's have a drink together!"

Some may be visited by ancestors from the Edo period or many generations back; but there is no need to worry if the Western food of today is a good choice to place in the altar. The ancestors fill up only through the steam; so the taste does not matter.

Also, during the 25 minutes of a food offering, it is also recommended that you sing ancestors' favorite songs, or sometimes tell them what their flaws were while they were alive, helping them make a realization. But listening to their flaws continuously and being told to reflect themselves may make them feel depressed. So I would like you to encourage them, saying: "I know you are now working very hard to atone for sins. Once you go up to the Spirit Realm, you will be able to come home besides mealtime, whenever you want."

On the other hand, if the descendants do not cook for them, the ancestors are left in hunger. If, in fact, the discipline is too hard for them to endure, it is possible they flee from the

Astral Realm. Gods will not stop them from escaping.

When escaping from the Astral Realm, the spirit will have to wander in this world as a wandering spirit. When this happens, the spirit is able to visit its decedents. For example, there are cases where an ancestor gets angry to see its descendants, saying, "Even though my descendants do not provide food in the altar, they are enjoying such delicious meals," and attaches himself to a descendant. In this case, the descendant will usually suffer from stomach or colon cancer, affecting the digestive system. Or even if not so serious, he/she will develop disorders, including weak digestion and loose bowels.

In this way, if you fail to offer proper services to your ancestors, there are many cases where descendants develop digestive disorders and eye trouble.

A man who developed a polyp in the stomach came to see me. I advised him to hold a memorial service for his ancestors; but instead he decided to undergo surgery to have the polyp removed. After the surgery, however, stomach cancer was found by the post-operative examination. He started giving up, saying: "I don't want to have surgery any more. I am old enough to accept the end of my life." I replied, "Your ancestor's spirit attaches himself to you, which caused the trouble to you. If you hold a memorial service for ancestors properly, you will be likely to get better." And I suggested to him about offering meals in the altar. Surprisingly, his cancer actually disappeared soon after he followed the suggestion.

If he had started memorial services for his ancestors at the onset of the polyp, I think he would not have developed cancer. By having to suffer more illnesses, he was taught the importance of a service for his ancestors.

No need to spend much money for family Buddhist alters and graves

There is no need to use money more than necessary on family Buddhist altars, graves, and offerings to the ancestors as well. For example, you can compare the altar to your home. The altar is where the ancestors come back every day to have a meal; so I think it should be cozy like the dining room or kitchen.

Also, the ancestors in the Spirit Realm are free to come to the altar anytime; so a welcoming altar is preferred to lavish grand altars.

As long as the doors are able to close, a simple, and reasonably priced altar would be fine. I also suggest installing some 6-watt fluorescent lights to brighten the inside to the perfect amount.

To those who come to me for counseling, I hand over a paper explaining these details. It is up to them whether to follow those instructions or not. If one thinks, "I already have an altar; I don't mind," then that is also fine.

Upon request, I also teach them how to pick up earthbound spirits. (I have added instructions on picking up earthbound spirits at the end of this chapter. Please refer to them.)

Although anyone is able to pick up these earthbound spirits, not everyone can admonish, guide, or get rid of them. If you bring the earthbound spirits collected by you to one of our lectures as introduced in the 2nd chapter, I will make them realize, and eliminate them accordingly after the lecture.

In fact, a grave is not a place where the spirits of the deceased get together. Until the 49th day after their death, they may be around their grave; but generally, the grave is not a place where you are able to meet the spirits. An altar is the place you can meet them. This is why I would like to emphasize your ancestors are not hoping for an extravagant, or a unique, grave, spending more money than necessary.

Recently graves in the form of an apartment are increasingly seen in cities. If you recall the deceased to your mind, cherishing the memories of them, the form of the grave does not matter. However, as long as you own a grave, it is crucial to keep it clean and well maintained, including thorough weeding. Bad spirits will unlikely to come to a clean place. (The meaning of visiting graves is also cleaning them.)

There are many more people spending excess amounts of money on memorial services for ancestors. Of course this may be due to the long and good relationships with their temples or neighbors. Ancestors also hope for better human relations. With this in mind, I suggest that you make well-balanced decisions, while avoiding damages on these relationships.

The ancestors in the Spirit Realm and the gods in the Realm of Deity will protect those who appropriately hold memorial services for their ancestors. The Spirit Realm is what is generally referred to as Heaven, and is the place where ancestors who have finished disciplines in the Astral Realm are supposed to go. The Realm of Deity is where deities abide. Once a human finishes the life cycle 30 times, he or she is able to become a god, and ascend to the Realm of Deity. In every family, there are ancestors who have ascended to this realm.

Ancestors who have ascended to gods protect offspring

I hear many people say, "My dead grandfather is protecting me"; but ancestors devoted to harsh discipline in the Astral Realm now cannot protect their descendents. It is your ancestors in the Spirit Realm or gods in the Realm of Deity that protect you. The ancestors in the Spirit Realm or gods in the Realm of Deity see their descendants sincerely holding services for the ancestors, which makes them think, "We should protect our descendants more." Since the spirits and gods have emotions as humans do, watching the descendants earnestly making offerings and praying for them with respect and reverence enhances their love toward their descendants.

Let me introduce you one example that shows how an ancestor ascended to a god protects his descendants.

There was a person who fell 7 meters at work. According to him, "The second I slipped off, my body floated and fell as if it were in slow motion." Upon reaching the ground, he fell with a thud. Falling from as high as 7 meters above the ground, surprisingly he was uninjured.

By making food offerings and praying for the ancestors sincerely every day, when their descendants are in danger, the ancestors will gently offer their helping hand.

As for me, I used to fall down the stairs quite often as a child; but I have never been hurt. Since I fell too many times, my parents decided to have the stairs carpeted. Just like the example I have mentioned, every time I fell, it was as if I had been hugged by something or someone, and floated, falling slowly and gently on the floor.

Here is another episode.

A woman driving on an expressway fell asleep at the wheel for an instant. The car veered off course to the shoulder of the road, bumping against it. However, the car was returned naturally to the center of the road, without a spin or rolling over. She said that it was as if someone had picked up her car and gently placed it on the lane.

Also there was a man who narrowly escaped being involved in a car accident while driving on a road. In his case, the

Chapter 1 Miracle Counseling

moment the car in front of him started to sway, it spun, jumping over the opposite lane. Then it crashed against the wall and eventually stopped. If the car had spun longer at that spot, he would have been badly involved in the accident. He was very lucky that the car bounced out into the opposite lane. Surprisingly, I heard the driver of the car was also uninjured.

Here is yet another case.

When someone was driving on the icy road, the car skidded and failed to stop on a downhill because the brakes didn't work properly. First it bumped against the pile of the snow on the road shoulder, bounced out into the opposite lane, again bumped against the snow on the opposite shoulder road, and finally stopped. Even though it was Sunday, there were no cars running on the opposite lane, and fortunately he was unhurt. Moreover, his car only sustained minor damage in one part of the headlight. All these good fortunes were brought by the gods of their ancestors who were always watching their daily services for their ancestors.

In talking about miraculous stories as these, we tend to conclude, "Our ancestors are protecting us." However, grandparents who passed away recently do not protect us; but ancestors who have ascended to gods do. With this in mind, I hope you to take good care of your ancestors, and hold proper memorial services in honor of them.

Also, ancestors do not want you to spend more money than

necessary on the Bon Festival (a Japanese Buddhist custom to honor the spirits of one's ancestors), the anniversary of their deaths, and anniversary memorial services. Your ancestors would be very happy to see you getting along with your family and relatives, gathering together and enjoying over a meal.

The chances of ancestors' souls being born as pets

Among questions about the services for ancestors, there is a topic I have been asked quite often recently. That is how to conduct services for pets. For family dogs and cats, their souls may belong to their original animals; or, in some cases, ancestors may have been reincarnated as dogs, cats, and very rarely rabbits.

If you bring me a photo of your pet to our lecture—preferably a photo of your pet facing the camera—I can tell you what kind of soul it is. From my experience, in many cases, the souls of family pets belong to those of ancestors.

The fact that human souls transmigrate into pets more often seems to be affected by the approaching of the end of this world. Also, there are cases where souls are made to be reborn in the form of pets from the Astral Realm with a view to making ancestors in the Beast Hell encourage realization and save their souls.

If you learn that your pets have the souls of your ancestors, I would like you to admonish them while taking good care of

Chapter 1 Miracle Counseling

them. A human soul usually is reincarnated as a human again. However, for example, a spy in the previous life may become a dog; or a mistress in the previous life may become a cat. Thus, please care for the pet, saying, "Be reborn as a human, next time." Then the ancestor is able to understand, and be guided accordingly.

Moreover, if the pet has a human soul, after the pet's death, I recommend you to name a posthumous Buddhist name, and make a memorial tablet for the services for your loved one.

〔How to pick up earthbound spirits〕

① In a transparent plastic bag, put about a bowlful of dirt, and tie the bag tightly. Please do not use a translucent bag or a sealable zipper bag. Please use a clearly transparent plastic bag,

② Hold the bag in your hand, and, while saying the following words, walk on the land you wish to pick up the earthbound spirits from.

"Earthbound spirits, I want to take you to a place of ease; so please get into the dirt in this bag."

Make sure of walking thoroughly through dark and narrow places inside and around the house, the corners of the rooms, and inside the closets, because those are spirits' favorite places. Please also go to the bathrooms, the entrance, the garden, and around the house outside. In addition, there could be spirits on the car; so please bring the bag and speak inside and outside of the car.

The spirits do not have a form, but have the same emotions as ours. So feel sincerely that you want these spirits to be saved, and please speak out to the spirits so that they can hear you. You will be able to pick up more spirits if you do the same at the same place on separate days about three times. If impossible, once or twice would be also fine.

③ **Without opening the bag, bring it with the collected spirits to our lecture, and please give it to the receptionists at the event. Then, the details on the next steps will be explained.**

※ **Please make sure of writing your name on the bag in ink.**

That is all for the way to pick up earthbound spirits.

If you bring the spirits to our lecture, I will admonish the spirits and guide them to an appropriate path, and,

Chapter 1 Miracle Counseling

for the evil spirits, I will cut and eliminate them. By picking up these earthbound spirits, problems, such as the followings, may be resolved: "There are eerie areas in the house"; "A family member is sickly"; "I have bad luck"; "The family is never at peace." (Since it depends on the cause, resdution is not guaranteed.) If you think this may apply, please try picking up these spirits at your home and your car.

Recently, I received a question from one of my blog readers, asking, "I was asked to pay 100,000 yen for the repose of the earthbound spirits, but is that reasonable?" It is never that expensive. As an appreciation to gods for the admonition and services for removing spirits, 5,000 yen is collected from those bringing in their bags of spirits. This is about the price for purification at a shrine. If asked for a very expensive fee, you should think it suspicious.

Earthbound spirits bring in several troubles to the home. A man, who came to our lecture in Tokyo, had had his house burned down. According to a god, it was not arson, but too many earthbound spirits in his home caused a fire. Even in arson cases, it has often something to do with the earthbound spirits.

"My family always has a problem"; "After moving, my health has gone bad"; "My family member is depressed";

"I have troubles in my work." These could be examples of earthbound spirits bringing bad luck. Another example of the presence of earthbound spirits would be hearing wrap-like sounds from a certain area in the house. This phenomenon could be resolved by picking up the earthbound spirits.

Chapter 2

Miracle Lectures

My guest appearances at the Miracle Lectures

Along with offering counseling as a spiritual counselor, I also give lectures as a guest speaker. In 2010, I made guest appearances as many as 19 times. I am continuously working energetically and touring across Japan every month this year, too.

With the theme "The truth never hitherto disclosed," the lecturer explains about "Why were we born and why are we here in this world?"; "What should we do to be happy?"; and "What will happen to the earth and human beings in future?"

Recently, there has been an increase in the number of unexpected incidents, such as parricides and filicides, which rarely happened in the past. In addition, we are facing quite a few problems, including larger natural disasters due to advancing global warming, and annual epidemics caused by new types of influenza.

In this chaotic state of life, many people seem to worry about their future and to lose their motivation for their lives. The lecturer talks with full of humor to the participants who are living in the present times, about the future of the earth and appropriate ways of life. I join the lectures as a guest speaker, playing a role of relaying the messages from gods.

I have experienced a number of psychic phenomena since I was a little girl. When I became a school girl, I came to be able to hear messages from gods. I was too young to recognize where

Chapter 2 Miracle Lectures

the voices were from at that time; but later I met the lecturer, and he taught me that the voices belong to gods.

Accepting the mission to pass on messages I receive from gods to people living in this current world, I am working as a spiritual counselor. I think the lecturer fully understands my mission and invites me to his lectures.

Besides relaying the messages from gods, I answer participants' questions and worries on the spot through communicating with gods (telepathic communication with gods). In this "channeling during the lecture," I ask gods for advice and answers for any kind of matters, such as wonders of this world which cannot be clarified by anybody including scientists, causes of intractable diseases and rare diseases which cannot be solved in medical science, and so on.

Specifically, the lecturer reads out the questions from participants, and I ask gods for advice, and then I relay them. As the truth of this world which is unknown to anybody can be clarified then and there, all the participants seem to be extremely surprised.

Any question is welcomed. I received the following questions in the previous lectures.

"When and with what seismic intensity will a Tokai earthquake and a major Tokyo earthquake (which directly hits the Metropolitan area) occur?"

"There are rumors going around about the world ending in 2012, and there is even a movie about the end of the world was released. Will the world really end?"

"Will Mt. Fuji erupt?"

"Abnormal weather has been one of the controversial issues recently, but will these weather conditions last for a while?"

"My son suffering from depression stays in hospital now. He doesn't seem to be recovering at all. What drove him into that situation? What should I do for him?"

"My daughter, a second year junior high school student, suddenly came to refuse to go to school. She avoids talking. What should I do?"

"What was Sakamoto Ryoma like?"

"Why are the bees disappearing all over the world?"

These are only a part of the questions that I answered. Besides these, I have received clear answers from gods for the facts of the incidents and accidents at issue, and future prospects of politics and economy. (Currently the number of the questions exceeds 100 in a single lecture, which has made me difficult to answer all. I apologize for this.) The details of the participants' questions and corresponding answers from gods will be shown in the next book I am planning to publish.

The lectures are also called "Miracle Lectures." A god direct-

Chapter 2 Miracle Lectures

ed me to name it in starting a guest appearance.

To be honest, I was uncertain whether or not miracles would actually happen. However, it soon ended up being a groundless doubt, because various miracles occurred one after another among the participants, saying, "I've got much better"; "I've recovered from a long-time chronic disease."

Here are a few episodes.

It happened at the lecture held in Gifu Prefecture on September 20, 2009. A woman suffering from a knee problem, who attended the lecture with her cane, left her cane behind after the lecture was over. Then, surprisingly enough, she walked home with a light step without her cane.

In another lecture, a man in a wheelchair suddenly stood up, and walked to the rest room during a recess. Seeing the miracle up close, his family members were extremely surprised. It is not rare that participants unbelievably recover from a long-standing headache or lower-back pain.

I have received many reports besides those about physical condition, as follows: "After attending your lecture, my company, on the verge of bankruptcy, started to improve"; "The relationship between wife and mother-in-law has improved a lot since we attended your lecture. We are getting along very well"; "I had been suffering from infertility for a long time, but just after your lecture, I got pregnant."

These are only a portion of the miracles. You might think:

"How could such a thing possibly happen?"; "I can't believe it." However, these miracles actually occurred. Gods are showing miracles to you, so that you can understand the fact that there exists an invisible world here, and that deities do exist in this world.

According to the organizer, the number of participants of the lectures has rapidly increased recently. I learned that whopping nearly 1,000 people attended the Gifu lecture in 2010.

As I have mentioned in the preface, my first book titled *WATARASE* seems to have contributed, more or less, to the rapid increase of the participants. Many of those who have read my book attended our lectures. In the autograph session held after each lecture, many participants say that reading my book brought them to the lecture. I am very grateful to them.

I started my personal official blog after publishing my book. There has been a good response to my blog, and, as well as my book, it also must be a contributing factor in increasing the lecture participants. About one third of the participants are likely to come to our lectures after reading my book and/or blog.

Thus, with an increasing number of participants, their age group seems to be changing. We used to have more elderly participants. The content of our lectures is about matters related to death, which might appeal to the heart of the elderly with experience of life and encourage them to listen very carefully.

Recently, however, younger people are increasingly attending our lectures. My blog and book must be playing an important role. Young people interested in spiritual things share their feelings with my book and blog, which may bring them to the lectures. I really realize that the number of those who have awakened their spirits (whose souls are aroused) is more constantly increasing than before.

This is the matter I am so much pleased with. If people try to think not with their brain, but feel and think with their heart (soul), I believe people will be able to return to what human beings should be.

The halls of the lectures are full of spirits

A large number of spirits gather together at our lectures. Then, how the spirits are taken to the halls? Let me explain the mystery.

First of all, when our lecture is held, among earthbound spirits and wandering spirits at that local area, only the spirits (souls) that will be possibly saved are assembled by gods to the hall. Earthbound spirits are disembodied people who died unnatural deaths such as those in accident, by suicide, by being murdered, during surgical operations, and in the bath. They have remained attached to the physical realm where they died, having unable to move on beyond a 50-meter radius. As a matter of fact, however, most earthbound spirits seem to feel too painful to move.

Wandering spirits, on the other hand, are spirits wandering this world without understanding their deaths, or unable to accept the fact that they died. Or they may have moved to the other world once only to return because of the hardship there. Every time our lecture is held, those spirits are taken to the hall all together.

It does not mean that all the earthbound spirits and wandering spirits at the local area are gathered. Among the spirits closely related to the participants, including their families, relatives, and friends, only the spirits that are allowed by gods are supposed to be assembled.

In the halls of our lectures, not only earthbound spirits and wandering spirits but the participants' ancestors also make their appearances. Unlike earthbound spirits and wandering spirits, those ancestors received their divine judgments on the 49th day after their deaths, and are now engaged in discipline in the Astral Realm. The Astral Realm, including hells, is where we are supposed to atone for our sins committed in the present life. Those ancestors who continuously do trying discipline are able to leave the Astral Realm temporarily with the permission from gods, and attend the lecture in which their offspring attend.

In this way, spirits closely connected with the participants are gathered at the hall. It sometimes happens that hundreds or

Chapter 2 Miracle Lectures

tens of thousands of spirits are related to a single participant. Therefore, the halls of our lectures are full of an amazing number of spirits.

When the spirits are taken to the hall, they are first gathered at the back of the hall. And then, as the starting time of the lecture draws near, they move to the front to listen to what a god explains.

I am not allowed to listen to their briefing. However, according to the spirits, it is not until that time that they realize they are taken to our lecture.

For instance, an earthbound spirit killed after being hit by a train came to the previous lecture, and I talked to the spirit. The spirit told me as follows: "The place I am bound to is very dim even in the daytime. The pain and agony I got the moment I was hit by the train continuously stay on and on. I was always praying that somebody would come to see me. One day, my field of vision suddenly expanded, and the next moment, I was surprised to find myself in this hall. I still didn't know what brought me here. Then, a god gave us an explanation, and I learned eventually that I was taken to this lecture hall."

Receiving an explanation from a god, the spirits move to the back where their families and relatives sit, and then listen to the lecture together with them while standing. Supposing that readers of this book attend our lecture, their dead family members and ancestors would listen to the lecture while standing at their back. I would like you to feel your loved ones, spirits behind you, when you attend the lecture. Participants increasingly came to feel the existence of the spirits, saying, "My shoulders feel light and warm"; "I feel my head is being pulled by somebody"; "My ears are ringing (many participants feel this way)." Even though spirits share the same space with us, they are in the 4-dimensional space, far away from us. Thousands of spirits, layered each other due to their lack of physical bodies, are able to enter the hall.

Some of you might feel scary to attend our lecture because of this large number of spirits; but do not worry. Spirits in the hall will never attach themselves to anybody, or never ever cause any trouble. Even if the spirits were to attach themselves to the participants to fulfill the mission by gods. they would stay only a few minutes and leave immediately after the completion of their mission. Gods never allow spirits to attach themselves to anybody any longer; therefore, participants cannot be possessed by spirits during our lectures.

Reasons why the hall is glittering gold

In the lecture hall, a considerable number of gods besides spirits gather together. When I talk on the stage, I sometimes feel that a god makes me talk through my body to relay the god's message. When I feel as if my body did not belong to me, a god is surely using my body.

Chapter 2 Miracle Lectures

Recently more participants have been able to feel the existence of gods. I can recognize this by their following comments: "The whole hall was glittering gold"; "Ms. Omori and the lecturer were covered with golden light, and their bodies emitted a rainbow-colored light"; "Purple and green balls of light were on the shoulders of Ms. Omori"; "On the side of the stage, I saw many golden figures frequently coming in and out of the hall."

The expressions vary from participant to participant, but it is indeed true that they were made to realize the existence of gods. The reason for this is that they were allowed to see the light of gods. The light of gods is gold on the whole, mixed with such as purple, green, and rainbow colors. The way to express it and how it looks like may differ with different participants.

Thus, the presence of a great number of gods leads the entire hall into being wrapped with beautiful golden and other colorful light. The fact that increasingly more people are coming to be able to see the light of gods also means that increasingly more people are coming to awaken their spirits, which is a wonderful thing. Furthermore, the halls and the areas where our lectures are held are clearly purified.

As seeing is believing, there are many that we cannot understand well without firsthand experiences. The reason people are shown such unusual phenomena is that gods are trying to let them notice the existence of gods in order to save them. This is well indicated by the fact that those who are not usually able to see spirits or who are not sensitive to spirits are allowed to see miracles before their eyes.

Reunion in tears with deceased family members

As I have already mentioned, a fair number of the spirits of the participants' families, relatives, and ancestors gather together in our lectures. Therefore, participants are sometimes allowed to meet their deceased family members during the lecture.

Here is one episode.

One of the questions I received in our lecture was, "Is it possible to know what my deceased wife is doing?" The moment I finished passing the message of a god for that question, a woman sitting in the first row started to cry loudly. As it happens, his deceased loved one came to the hall, and attached herself to the woman in the first row.

Since it happened during the lecture, an oppressive atmosphere suddenly pervaded the hall. However, I did not know where the husband was in the hall packed with nearly 1,000 participants. Then, the lecturer said: "Where is the husband? Meet your wife if you want." And then, a man raised his hand, approaching the crying woman.

On seeing the man, the woman hugged him and just kept crying. Giving her hand a firm squeeze, the man consoled the

Chapter 2 Miracle Lectures

spirit of his wife. For a while, they spent their own time together with their hands held tightly. People in the hall were warmly watching over their moving reunion. In a flash, the atmosphere of the hall became one with all of the participants, giving them a sense of togetherness and true love.

After the lecture, the man came to the staff to express his thanks: "The woman was, to be sure, my wife. I am glad to attend the lecture, and I really appreciate it."

Here is another episode in our another lecture

A couple asked a question: "We are always worried about our son we lost in an accident a few years ago. We wish to know what he is doing in the other world."

While I was relaying the message of a god to them on the stage, I could see a pale light coming down gently behind the couple. Watching closely, I saw a spirit emitting a blue light like a spotlight. Soon I recognized that the spirit must be the son the couple mentioned, and that the couple must be the ones sitting in front of the spirit.

I quite often see pale lights while I am reading gods' messages. I usually do not mention, but I somehow told the lecturer that I spotted their son inadvertently.

Then he said to me loudly enough to be heard to all the audience: "Oh, you seem to know where the son is now in this hall. Why don't you let his parents know about it?" I was afraid that my calling to the son's parents among a large audience might make them feel embarrassed as he passed away in the accident, but I convinced myself it would work positive, and then asked the couple sitting in front the spirit spotted with light, "You are the parents of the deceased son, aren't you?" "Yes, we are," replied the couple.

Some of my readers might doubt that I read their facial expressions, but it was absolutely impossible. The hall was too large with a capacity audience of 1,000 to identify each facial expression from the stage.

After the lecture, the couple came to see me at the autograph session in order to express their gratitude. The spirit of their son was still standing behind them, and I relayed his messages to them, including: "When I died, I felt this way"; "If I lived longer, I could do this and that"; "I still have lingering attachment to such and such a thing in this world." These were what I could never ever be able to know. Listening to his messages carefully, his father started to shed tears.

Later I learned from the couple's friend that he never cries in the presence of others. He must have been moved to tears by his reunion with his loved one and his messages, firmly believing that the spirit was his own son.

Here is another episode in our lecture held in a local area.

I received a question from a woman asking me what her daughter lost in an accident is doing. A pale spotlight came down to one spot in the hall as well. Though I soon recognized

Chapter 2 Miracle Lectures

the sprit spotted with light was the daughter of the questioner, I read her mother's heart to mean that she didn't want to disclose things about her daughter to the audience.

The lecturer called out to the audience: "Where is a questioner? If you do not mind, raise your hand, and you can meet your daughter again." Her mother, however, was vacillating in raising her hand or not: "What shall I do? Unless I identify myself as her mother, I won't be able to see her, but I don't want anybody to know . . ." Then I continued to read the message of a god after I said to the lecturer, "Her mother is now hesitating; so it would be better not . . ."

Nevertheless, the woman wanted to see her daughter. When I was thinking it would be great if she was able to see her daughter, she came to the autograph session after the lecture. I soon recognized her as the mother of the deceased daughter.

Then, I talked to her, "Let's meet your daughter now." Naturally enough, she was surprised saying, "How did you know I am the mother of her?" I explained to her: "Your daughter was standing behind you during the lecture. Feeling that you don't want to be identified, I was intentionally talking toward the different direction from you." She looked even more surprised, and said, "I was exactly thinking that way!"

After the autograph session was over, I arranged their reunion. I made the spirit come through the body of a female member of staff and talk with the mother. After sharing a precious time with her daughter, she looked so happy and rejoiced from her heart, saying: "I confirmed the truth that I had long wanted to ask my daughter. What had been weighing on my mind was gone, and I feel at ease now. This reunion greatly encouraged me to go forward. I can't thank you enough."

We have more cases of touching reunion at the venue of our autograph session. A woman coming to the autograph session asked me what her dead father had been doing. Then I said to her, "He is just behind you now." Soon after that, his spirit entered a female member of staff standing there. The female staff to whom the spirit was attached started to talk as if she had been quite a different person, a man. Then the reunion in tears with her father was realized there. It was her first time in 30 years to meet her father, and this meeting was allowed by gods.

These unexpected moving reunions can never be intentionally arranged by me. Only in the case that gods allow, the reunion with their loved ones can be realized.

Parting with your loved ones is a real wrench. Here is a message from a god as to parting.

A message from a god

Parting with physical bodies . . .
It is quite natural that you feel sorrowful

if you lose your loved ones.
There are many who can hardly get over their pain.
Especially those who have lost their family members
including parents, children, brothers, sisters, and their spouses
are overwhelmed with grief.
Most of them cannot believe or accept their deaths.
However, they themselves should go forward,
accepting the reality as it is.
Humans are born with the gift for that.
If you, who live in this world, continuously lament over the
death of your loved one, going on grieving and being depressed,
further misfortune will be brought upon you.
People who died, whatever the cause or reason may have been,
have gone to the 4-dimensional space ahead of you
for atonement after the completion of their life practice.
Nothing has changed but the place to train them.
Everything is just the same with you
except that they do not have physical bodies.
They have consciousness.
They have rather returned to what a human being should be.
The true figure of a human being is not the one
with a physical body,
but one's consciousness without a physical body.
When you are in this material world, the 3-dimensional space,
however, you feel scary to lose your physical body.

Your physical body is not everything.
After you leave your physical body behind,
you will enjoy an indefinably refreshing sense of liberation.

A message from a god

You should not lament over the death of people.
The deceased prefers being seen off cheerfully
on his/her journey to the afterlife
rather than with a lot of tears of sorrow.
If they cry loudly, the deceased also feels like crying.
The deceased even feels very painful
wondering if he/she did something horrible.
The day of the funeral can spiritually be translated
as an auspicious day because people can eventually set out
on a journey to the next realm for discipline
after completing this life.
It is the day to take one step forward to a god.
(As a human being is able to become a god
after they complete their lives 30 times.)
On such an auspicious day,
however hard they cry and cling to the deceased,
saying "Don't leave me behind!"
the deceased feels irritated for being unable to do anything
and sorry for dying before them.

Chapter 2 Miracle Lectures

Confused by mixed feelings,
the deceased cannot easily start on a journey,
which may result in the attachments to this world.
Worried about family and friends left behind,
the deceased cannot fully enjoy himself/herself
in the other world. (The 4-dimensional space.)
Let him/her rest in peace.
It would be better to encourage the deceased by saying:
"You don't have to worry about us in this world.
Hang in there with your mind at ease!"
It may sound very frank, but it will help the deceased
remove his/her attachments to this world.
This is what the bereaved are supposed to do as their role.

It happens all of a sudden that the spirits enter the bodies of the participants and staff members. Therefore the whole audience seems very surprised to see the scene. There are several TV programs featuring spiritual matters arranged and well organized in advance. A series of events that happen during our lectures, however, are never arranged beforehand as a matter of course. It is no wonder that they get extremely amazed to see the miracles because they happen on the spot on the spur of the moment.

In addition to the spirits of a family's loved ones, those of great figures including historical figures can be evoked during our lectures. The audience is allowed to ask any question or mystery except matters that gods judge as premature to disclose.

In our previous lecture, gods allowed me to evoke the spirit of Oda Nobunaga, and I got the spirit to enter the body of a woman. Then, her expression, particularly a look in her eyes dramatically changed, which was just like that of Oda Nobunaga. The whole audience seemed to be amazed to see her. And then, I got Nobunaga himself to tell what actually happened in his days, the truth of the history.

In this way, evoking the spirit of an actual great figure makes it possible to verify the truth that cannot possibly be disclosed. I myself often find it astonishing to hear the stories that might require us to revise history.

In our lecture held in Fukushima Prefecture, the spirits of a military unit of the Aizu domain called "Byakko-tai (or White Tigers)" were taken to the hall, and they were standing straight at the back very politely. Those spirits of still young Byakko-tai members were watching the stage with serious looks. Of course I informed the audience of their spirits appearing in the hall.

Thus, our lectures, where a great number of spirits gather together, play a significant role as a place to meet their loved ones and listen to what historical figures talk about which is otherwise absolutely impossible to learn. Just to be sure, let me repeat that it never happens that spirits attach themselves to

Chapter 2 Miracle Lectures

you just because you attend our lectures. You do not have to worry about it.

Your attendance at the lectures saves souls

The spirits attending our lecture are carefully listening to what the lecturer talks about, standing behind their families and relatives. Even if the participants doze off, the spirits behind them are listening attentively with sincere attitudes, which will help facilitate their spiritual realization.

Earthbound spirits are those who have not received their divine judgments and are still unable to cross over to the Astral Realm. Many of wandering spirits, as well, have not received their divine judgments only to fail to move to the Astral Realm. Not a few of such wandering spirits are still unaware of their deaths. It is not until they listen to our lecture that they realize their deaths, and that they become enlightened.

Or, some wandering spirits understand their deaths, but refuse to receive their divine judgments because of their strong attachment to this world. Those spirits not only wander this world, but also attach themselves to people. However, it is regarded as a sin to take possession of people. By listening to our lectures, those wandering spirits are able to get rid of their attachment, which encourages them to accept their deaths. Consequently, they come to understand that taking possession of a living person is a sin.

In this way, wandering spirits are able to be admonished by listening to the stories at our lectures. On deciding to go to the Astral Realm after receiving their divine judgments, they start to leave the bodies of people. In fact, quite a few spirits set out on a journey to the Astral Realm after being admonished at our lectures.

On the other hand, in the case of ancestor spirits, their soul stage will be raised every time they listen to the stories at our lecture. Let me give you one specific example. I had a chance to talk with a spirit, who had been working hard to atone for her sins amidst great suffering in the Lake of Blood, one of the hells of the Astral Realm, before she came to visit our lectures. Several chances to attend our lectures seem to have enlightened her. She said: "On returning to the Astral Realm, I was surprised to find myself landed in a different place. Now I am free from pain, and engaged in weeding." The teaching at our lectures enlightened her, which led to raise her soul level, and eventually changed the place of her atonement in the other world.

In this way, a number of spirits are admonished and guided at our lectures, leaving human bodies. That is to say, your participation to our lectures can be a great contribution toward saving a great number of spirits.

Most of the participants think that they attend our lectures for their own sake. If they learn the truth that they are taking

Chapter 2 Miracle Lectures

spirits to the lecture and also saving those spirits, they will find it more significant to attend our lectures.

Among the first-time participants, there are some who are invited by their friends, and attend our lectures without much thought. Or, some others may be forced to attend the lectures against their will. Whatever the reason is, your act of attending our lecture in itself is equivalent to saving people.

If you attend our lectures, it follows that your ancestors are taken there. And then, you save a great many spirits after all without knowing it, which is also regarded as a contribution to deities.

Only one evening meal together with ancestors

As I mentioned, after the spirits that are taken to our lectures make a realization, they will go on a journey to the Astral Realm, leaving the humans they attached themselves to. Among those who have achieved realization, however, some spirits are allowed by gods to spend only a night at their family house.

In most cases, after the spirits are admonished and guided properly, they start to leave the human bodies, heading for their divine judgments first. However, the time for divine judgments is fixed in the morning. That's the reason why gods allow the spirits to stay at their family house only that night.

Particularly for the earthbound spirits who come to our lecture after being released, it might be their first reunion in several decades. Therefore, it must be a warm arrangement of gods to let them spend dinner time together with their family, even a single night. In some case, gods allow spirits to stay with their family for a week, as the replacement of a memorial service on the 49th day after their death.

I always ask the family of those spirits who have received permission from gods to have dinner with their ancestors that night.

I would like those family members to prepare dinner for their ancestors, and arrange the dining table, sharing the meal and time together. This is the meal set for the deceased called "kagezen" in the old days. I would like to advise them to prepare the meal, sit around the table together with their ancestors, and talk to them: "Let's eat together"; "How do you like being at home after a long interval?"

Nevertheless, the portion of the meals of the ancestors will never be finished even after they eat together, because spirits do not eat from the mouth but fill their stomach by inhaling the steam from the dishes.

Even though the dishes for the ancestors remain the same after they enjoy eating them, the taste of the food will change. Specifically, in the case that sushi is offered, the flavor of vinegar is likely to be lost. My blog readers often report that they find the taste quite different. If you have opportunities to share meals with your ancestors, remember to compare the taste of the dishes for your family with the one for your ancestors after the meals are offered. Many people seem to recognize the difference. To be frank, you will find them unpalatable, in most cases, lacking flavor.

The toxins of the parts possessed by spirits start to melt

I mentioned that, if attaching spirits are admonished and guided properly, they start to leave the human bodies. This is technically called "separation of spirits." The scene of separation of spirits is so beautiful that it looks as if the whole hall were wrapped with fantastic light.

Do you know a creature, a sea butterfly, named *Clione limacina*? As the name is believed to be from the sea sprite (Muse of history) "Clio" in Greek myths, *Clione* is very beautiful like an angle of floating ice. The scene that a large number of spirits start to separate from the bodies of the participants in the lecture hall is as beautiful as *Clione* swimming up to the sea surface, shimmering in the water. I am so mesmerized by the mystical beauty that I almost forget about the time.

When the spirits start to leave the bodies, some people feel their heart twitch. Others feel restless or a little pain. These are nothing to worry about.

In many cases, chronic illnesses are cured by the separation of the long possessed spirits. The reason for this is that the toxin builds up in the part of the body where the spirits attached themselves, and starts to melt little by little when the spirits start to leave. This is the very reason why our lectures are called "Miracle Lectures": as a matter of fact, many miracles, including recuperation from illness and improvement in life, often happen.

Most of the causes of the disease have something to do with spiritual interference. For example, intractable diseases without known causes, such as cancer, psychological disorders, depression, and dementia, are caused by something spiritual in many cases, according to a god. Also, most of the causes of misfortune, such as family trouble and criminal damage, are thought to be due to spiritual interference.

It is difficult to completely get rid of the spiritual problem which is the root cause of diseases and misfortunes. However, by attending our lectures, attaching spirits are admonished, are guided, and leave the bodies of the participants, which eventually could resolve regular health problems and improve their lives.

As a condition for a miracle, however, you should accept the content of our lecture with an open mind. Your poor physical condition could also be related to your own heart besides spiritual matters. Therefore, unless you reflect on your past behavior deeply or change your way of living, you will never be helped out of your difficult situation even after the spirits leave your body.

Chapter 2 Miracle Lectures

"I reluctantly attended the lecture as my friend invited me, but I can't accept such a story."

"If a person dies, everything is over. That's it. So, what's wrong with living as I like?"

As long as you do not renew your way of thinking as these, you will fail to experience a miracle.

I do not mean to push you to obediently follow what the lecturer says, but I hope you to accept the content first whether you follow or not, reflect on your behavior, understand that this world is the place of life practice, and then make efforts to change your way of living. Improving your mindset is most important.

Here is a message from a god showing the importance of accepting the truth.

A message from a god

We are always sharing messages with everyone equally.
Unfortunately many people do not notice them.
We are giving you messages in detail about something
from future predictions to individual matters every day.
Without any fogginess on your soul,
you could immediately receive our messages here
even without any gift of special ability.
We wish all human beings would accept our messages.

Now we only send messages to you telepathically.
However, at the end of this civilization,
we will send individual telepathic messages to each of you
so that the messages can be reached and heard.
Whether you obediently follow the voice and trust us,
or insist on your thoughts,
poses a crossroads of a turning point in your life.
This could be the last chance
to decide whether you believe in us or not.
We do hope you keep in mind that the day,
when you will come to hear the messages from us in person,
is drawing near.
It is coming in near future . . .

A message from a god

"Those who believe shall be saved."
You may have heard this adage many times,
but few people understand the true meaning of it.
Many of you fail to understand
"those who believe what shall be saved."
That's why you may believe what you should not,
and follow a different path from our wish.
What we want you to acknowledge and believe is the truth that
we, special beings in higer-dimensional spaces, called gods,

Chapter 2 Miracle Lectures

do exist.
Many of you may think
that this 3-dimensional space is the only realm in this world,
but that is wrong.
Many of you may think
that your physical bodies are your original figures,
but they are only like containers that you use in this world.
The true self is not in your physical body,
but in your consciousness.
That's the reason your consciousness is able to
change your physical body.
You can do it easily, just by thinking in your consciousness.
Anyone can do it.
If you do not want to get sick, for example,
you should just make up your mind not to get sick.
With that in mind, you should lead a life.
That is all.
If you are suffering from a disease,
you should be conscious of the part being recovered.
Then, you should believe you will surely get recovered.
That's it . . .
You do not have to make things complicated.
Everything is so simple.
Try to think things more simply.
Believe in special beings called gods and act accordingly,

and you will be able to be in harmony with energy of this universe.

Various miracles occurring to the participants of the lectures

What miracles are actually happening at our lectures? Let me give you some concrete examples.

I have already shown a few examples of the miracles that happened during, or after, our lectures. One person came to our lecture with a cane, but went home, leaving it behind. The other person suddenly stood up from the wheelchair, and walked unassisted by anyone. Besides them, I have received various miraculous stories from the participants. Here are more examples.

★ (A female in her 70s) It was my 3rd time to attend your lectures. I received the power of the universe into my body, and I felt so hot that its hotness continued while I was in the train on my way back home. I suffer from Parkinson's disease, but I became able to go up and down stairs after receiving the power of the universe. I walked back home with lighter steps.

★ (A female in her 60s) My lower-back pain for years was reduced by the power of the universe, and my back started stretching out gradually. Now my whole body straightens out, and I feel much better. Thank

Chapter 2 Miracle Lectures

you so much.

★ (A female in her 60s) My shoulder pain was removed, and I felt much lighter. It's been 9 days since your lecture, but I still do not feel any pain at all.

★ (A female in her 60s) My gums were too painful to eat anything except soft food for the last one year. Even my dentist couldn't help me. Since I attended your lecture, however, the pain has unbelievably gone, and now I am enjoying eating any kind of food. Thank you very much.

★ (A female in her 60s) I had poor circulation, and my feet always felt very cold, which often deprived me of a good night's sleep. Since I had my body filled with the power of the universe, I have been feeling warm, down to my toes. I can sleep soundly until morning, thanks to the power. It's been a great help to me.

★ (A male in his 30s) I had painful stiff shoulder and lower back. My experience of the power of the universe has dramatically relieved the pain.

★ (A female in her 40s) I was concerned about my mother's advancing dementia, and decided to attend your lecture. Then I found her facial expression changed for the better just after the lecture. She looks like the way she used to be. The way she speaks is more natural. I am so happy to see her change. Thank you so much.

Listening to the stories from the participants, I have found those who have health problems are more likely to witness the miracles better. I realize people with poor health seem to experience more dramatic miracles. That's because their changes are more noticeable.

People with excellent health, on the other hand, might not see miracles so clearly because their changes are more subtle.

People in good health sometimes say: "I felt hot"; "My vision cleared up, and I could see much better." Especially when they are attached by spirits, their vision can be affected. By removing bad spirits, their field of vision might regain the clarity.

Cleansing reaction is the sign of recovery

Some of those who really realize the experience of miracles temporarily get out of condition after our lectures. This, what we call "cleansing reaction," is not a matter to worry about. Then, let me give you some examples of those reactions.

When the attaching spirits start to leave you, the poison of some parts of your body begins to dissolve, which sometimes causes you to feel pain at those parts. Also, you may have loose bowels, or vomit due to detoxifying effects. There are, moreover, cases of cleansing reaction as follows:

Chapter 2 Miracle Lectures

◎ After your lecture, I felt so listless.
◎ After your lecture, I had a nosebleed.
◎ After your lecture, my headache became worse.
◎ After your lecture, my lower-back pain became more painful.
◎ After your lecture, I came out in a rash, and my atopic dermatitis got worse.

If you temporarily have these symptoms after attending our lectures, you can take them as the evidence that the attaching spirits start to leave your body, and that the poison begins to dissolve accordingly. Cleansing reaction is, so to speak, a good sign of recovery of your physical condition.

Particularly at our lecture in Gifu Prefecture in 2010, quite a few participants seem to have experienced cleansing reactions, because the lecturer and I removed almost all the attaching bad spirits who were the least likely to make realization.

Grudges and obsessions of human spirits and animal spirits are sometimes too strong to leave even after they are admonished. Then, a god emits light through a human body, eradicating the souls of those evil spirits in a flash.

While you are having your spirits removed, you never feel pains or itchy. In the case of our lecture in Gifu Prefecture, since the long attaching spirits started to leave, the more participants showed cleansing reactions.

The cleansing reaction, however, soon calms down. I can not specify its exact period due to differences between individuals, but generally it only lasts from one day to one week, at the longest. After that reaction is over, most people feel better, getting back into shape.

In my case, for instance, as a symptom of the cleansing reaction of the melting poison, a nettle rash broke out exactly for five days all over my body, surprisingly except for the exposed parts like the face, hands, feet, and legs. On the morning of the 6th day, the rash was completely gone, and my body felt lighter, getting back into shape.

More surprisingly, my daughter came out in hives in turn the moment my cleansing reaction was over. My daughter's rash was, strange enough, also gone completely after five days, exactly the same as my case. Still more curiously, the next turn was my son, who had hives, and, just the same as our cases, completely recovered after five days.

Later a god told me our hives were due to the medicine I took several times during the breast-feeding period and amazingly the poison started to melt in the form of hives.

As I mentioned so far, after participating our lectures and having your spirits removed, you may have cleansing reactions. However, they do not occur to everyone. Those who accept the content of our lectures seriously are more likely to experience these reactions. This does not mean that people without cleansing reactions did not listen to our lectures seriously. Reactions vary from person to person. Therefore, I would like you to take this just as the way of suggestion.

A psychiatrist attends the lectures

Various people attend our lectures: those who are suffering from intractable diseases and misfortunes, struggling with distress in their lives, those whose family members or friends are in poor condition, and those whose jobs are related to spirituals.

As I have already mentioned, a psychiatrist attended our lecture before. When I asked what brought him to the lecture, he replied, "There are some mental disorders that are absolutely impossible for the current medical science to clarify." Patients with various symptoms visit the psychiatric department. "I cannot but think that some of their mental conditions must have been caused by matters, not in their present life but in their past life," he continued, "Realizing the limitations of medical science, I cannot find any way but prescribe the regular medicine."

Those psychological disorders cannot be clarified or recovered by medication. Some psychiatrists realize this situation, struggling in the dilemma. Some doctors even advise those patients to ask for help to spiritual counselors.

Not only a psychiatrist but an osteopath took a young woman and her mother to me. The osteopath said: "Her depression does not show any improvement even though she received treatment at the hospital. Her doctor advised her to visit an osteopathic clinic for a change of air, and came to my clinic. Her case is beyond me, or any medical care is of no use. So, as the last hope, I took her to you. I do hope she will be getting better."

The osteopath had been one of the readers of my blog, and trusted me, saying, "I've known you through your blog, and I have no doubt of your spiritual power." After conducting spiritual investigation, I removed her attaching spirits on the spot.

There are also some cases that patients with terminal cancer or intractable diseases visit me for consultation. Some of those suffering from terminal cancer are advised to go to spiritual counselors as there is nothing to be done in the field of medical service. As cancer is beyond cure, how they seek for peace of mind may be the most important factor for them.

The miracles that people experience at our lectures cannot be explained in the current medical science, that's why our lectures are called "Miracle Lectures."

Long queues at the autograph sessions

As our lectures have not widely been advertised, many participants used to find out about them on the flyers distributed

Chapter 2 Miracle Lectures

by the organizer or by word of mouth, or used to be invited by their friends and family. Recently, however, more and more people came to know our lectures through my blog and book, and decide to attend them.

Some first-time participants seem to feel a little nervous, wondering what our lecture is like. However, after the lecture, to my surprise and joy, most of them give me a word of thanks: "I am so happy to have attended your lecture. Thank you so much." Let me show some of the comments I received from the participants, as follows.

★ (A female in her 40s) I reflected on my life, thoughts, and my way of living in the past. "I want to be happy. Why am I always suffering from emotional pain in this world?" This question used to be in my mind. Listening to your lecture, I've made up my mind to change my self-consciousness. I hope I will be able to improve myself, and I will continue to attend your lectures in order to go forward.

★ (A female in her 60s) What you lectured about was the most basic and crucial for human beings. I was impressed. Though I tend to be swept along by daily life, I found it important to make utmost efforts to live a moral life, always conscious of my pure heart and good behavior. I learned a lot from your lecture.

★ (A female in her 40s) Thank you very much for an instructive lecture. I think I can spend my days with a different frame of mind from today. I will talk about your lecture to my husband.

★ (A female in her 40s) I can't say thank you enough. I am most grateful to my friend for inviting me to your lecture.

★ (A male in his 60s) I will live a life in gratitude. I thank my son's wife for taking me here. Thank you.

★ (A female in her 50s) I used to put the blame on somebody else when I met a mishap. I learned, however, I am to blame for those, and my way of thinking will change things for the better. Though it may take a little time to put that into practice, I will keep your story in my mind, and spend my daily life with thanks. Thank you very much.

★ (A female in her 20s) I was taken to your lecture by my mother. Unexpectedly I was moved. So far, I caused a lot of trouble to the people around me; so from now, I'll do all I can for others.

Similar comments to these, I also receive quite often at the autograph sessions after our lectures. Since I started autograph sessions after lectures, in addition to the regular ones just after publishing my 1st book, many people have lined up at the hall.

Chapter 2 Miracle Lectures

When the lecture is held at a large hall, they sometimes wait in long queues over 2 hours. In that case, I can hardly have enough time to talk with each of them. They express, regardless of only a short-time exchange between us, warm and heart-felt thanks to me.

At my autograph sessions, I shake hands with the participants while filling them with the power of the universe. Those who feel the power in shaking hands say: "My body feels hot"; "My hands are pricking." Once, an elderly person whom I met at my autograph session said: "It used to be really hard for me to keep on standing even for 10 minutes due to my leg pain. Strangely enough, I have been standing for an hour, waiting for my turn for your autograph, but I feel no pain at all."

Sometimes autograph sessions are extended longer. However, surprisingly enough, they end just on time when we are supposed to leave the hall.

This is true of the lecturer. He sends the power of the universe to the participants at our lectures. "Sending the power of the universe" means to cleanse people's bodies. More specifically, it is to emit the light of God from the palm of the hand, which will help alleviate the pains and conditions of the diseases, and dissolve poison in the bodies. Many participants wait in a line for their turns to experience the power of the universe. This session, just like the autograph session, ends precisely on the closing time.

A god instructs us to hold autograph sessions, and send the power of the universe to the participants. A god might adjust time, and make the session end on time so that we may not cause any trouble to the people concerned.

People are reaching out for the lectures

I have been joining the lectures for the past few years as a guest speaker, and recently I strongly came to realize people are reaching out for them.

Since all the seats are non reserved seats (reserved seats may be available in some halls in the near future), halls used to be occupied from the back seats. However, recently, the halls start to be filled from the middle seats of the front line. Furthermore, they begin to wait in a line 1 hour prior to reception, running into the hall for good seats the moment the door is opened. People coming after them find a handkerchief placed on one of those seats, and ask if it is taken, which has become a common scene at our recent lectures.

While I am speaking on the stage, I often see the participants, sitting in the front row, lean forward, breathing in every word. This is what I had never seen in our previous lectures. I am surprised to find the great change of atmosphere of our lectures.

As I mentioned before, young people have increasingly started to join our lectures. Junior high school students came to

Chapter 2 Miracle Lectures

the autograph session after our lecture, and I asked them if they understood the lecture. Then, they replied: "Yes, we did. We enjoyed your lecture a lot." Probably more and more young people have come to show interest in the invisible world.

Some readers of my blog are able to see spirits. Many of them have kept their abilities secret, regarding the abilities as matters not to be disclosed. Reading my blog, in which you can find many readers who believe in the world invisible to the human eye, they seem to come to realize that they can talk about spiritual stuff, which helps them feel at ease. Those who are worried about their being sensitive and receptive in a spiritual sense are likely to feel relieved to read my blog.

Unexpectedly, so many people have come to our lectures and read my blog. This must be the proof that our souls are connected. Appreciating my soul connection with them, I will continuously relay gods' words to you through lectures, books, and blogs.

I received a god's message about the situation that people increasingly come to show interest in the world invisible to the human eye. I do hope the following message will be of some help to you.

A message from a god

*Originally, people with physical bodies did not have to know
things besides their present world (the 3-dimensional space).
People are born
after their memories of their past life were completely erased,
because they do not need to know anything
about the different dimensional spaces.
People's souls, however, have been being evolved greatly, and
they are beginning to realize the different dimensional spaces.
More people are interested in their past life and after life.
So, the time, we should tell the truth accurately, has come.
We will instruct you exactly
so that there might be no misunderstanding.
We will use people who can correctly relay our messages to you.
The souls of those who carefully listen to them
have already reached that high level.
Nevertheless, you should not criticize, or despise, those
who fail to listen.
Their souls are still young.
They have not reincarnated so often yet.
That's why they cannot accept our messages so easily.
They would be all right
because they will eventually accept them without fail*

Chapter 2 Miracle Lectures

when the time is ripe.
People with their souls aroused should lead the people
with younger souls.
Be sure not to be forcible to them.

On March 13, 2011, a god allowed me to take the spirits of 180 victims (particularly in Iwate Prefecture), who were swallowed up by the tsunami of the 3.11 Great East Japan Earthquake in 2011, to a place in Gifu Prefecture. And then, together with about 250 persons, we listened to how they felt while sharing their pains. I advised them to realize the situation, and how to cope with things thereafter.

There were so many spirits wondering—those who were choked with a large amount of mud, children screaming in pain with his leg torn off, a mother calling her children's names in panic with some stuff coming out of her cracked head . . . It was just like the disaster-stricken area where the victims passed away, an extremely devastating, as well as terrifying, sight.

Many of them seemed to have thought of themselves still alive. Not knowing what had happened to them, they were just screaming without accepting the harsh reality. I felt so overwhelmed and sorry for them that I explained what had occurred to them while crying in sorrow.

Not a few of them died at different places from their family members, and met again on those spots. Seeing their family reunions, I was moved by their tight family bond.

The profound love of gods and the very cooperative persons eventually released all the 180 spirits from their suffering, making their astral bodies (the bodies to be used after death) comfortable. After their divine judgments, they fortunately left for the next world without becoming earthbound spirits.

The same event happened at the special seminar held on March 27, 2011. Gods took, and saved, 300 spirits of those who have yet to be found since they perished in Miyagi Prefecture in the wake of the Great East Japan Earthquake.

When the seminar started, many of those spirits gathered at the front of the stage, shivering with cold and screaming, "I am freezing." Some of them collapsed on the stage, and others joined their hands in prayer, asking for help in agony.

As the seminar went on, they came to calm down. They seemed to understand the situation eventually, and I saw their looks of agony fading away. I felt relieved and very glad to see their change.

Epilogue

The time has come for the Japanese to be awaken to their mission

*The unprecedented Great East Japan Earthquake
with a magnitude of 9.0 on the Richter scale.
We are watching, how people like you living in Japan
see, view, and act to cope with this disaster,
which will lead to change your lives hereafter.
People, living their lives in Japan this time,
with special missions,
have been tested and disciplined considerably by us.
Japan is a country of God,
which has been unchanged since the earth was created.
Even when the continent of Mu sank into ocean,
Japan was left, and you were there at that time.
You may not remember at all, but at that time
you were astonished to see most parts of the huge continent
sinking to the bottom of the sea.
Then we told you that the continent of Mu
would emerge again in tens of thousands of years.
We also told you that those living in this land (the present
Japan) are destined to play a leading role in the same way
in an effort to save the earth once again.
And the time has just come at last.
The continent of Mu,
once a thriving continent during the Mu Empire era,
will emerge from the Pacific Ocean
as a result of a huge tectonic movement,*

Epilogue: The time has come for the Japanese to be awaken to their mission

whereas, some towns (land) will sink to the bottom of the ocean.
Atlantis will also emerge.
In China and Africa, there will be huge geological faults
over 1,000 kilometers.
Continents will be damaged so badly
as some of them might be severed.
After the tectonic movement,
the world's topography will dramatically change,
leading to change the world map, of course,
and the map of Japan as well.
You were born, with your soul aspiring for this revolution.
It is your soul that desired it.
Nobody is to blame. This is what you decided.
Your soul is, without doubt, strong enough
to overcome the planned future events.
Arouse your soul.
Now is the time you should be spiritually awaken.
You should awake to your mission.
Together with us, give love to those who hanker after love,
saving their souls.
Your soul desires to do the salvation.
You will find it fulfilling and meaningful for your life.
Put aside your trifling desires and pride, and be constantly on
the move just for saving and helping people.
To help people release from their pains

will surely bring the foremost pleasure to you.
You should help a number of people lead
to the would of God's light.
You can do it, without fail . . .
We are absolutely sure you can do it.
We have been looking forward to this moment.
This is a matter of great pleasure.
You should enjoy this pleasing and precious moment.
You have only to change your way of thinking.
Take it, "It's so fun!"
Anyone with the mission can do it.
Well, let's get the show on the road!

This is a message I received from a god in the wake of the Great East Japan Earthquake on March 11, 2011. A large number of people perished in this disaster, and lost their loved ones or their houses. All of Japan was engulfed by grief.

"Japan is a country of God, and is supposed to be protected; but why did such a catastrophic disaster as this occur?" many people may have wondered why. Responding to this, a god explained "Since Japan is a country of God, it was necessary to awaken the souls of those in Japan, and band people together."

We should never forget the pains of those who were killed in that earthquake, and the deep grief of those who lost their families or friends. Understanding the bitter decision to make

Epilogue: The time has come for the Japanese to be awaken to their mission

for God, the hearts of the people of Japan should be one. It is crucial to overcome this difficulty, and move forward to a bright future.

A god also says, "When the hearts of the Japanese become one, there will be a plan to strengthen their solidarity on a global scale." On that account, an asteroid might possibly approach the earth, and the asteroid in the worst-case scenario could collide with the earth, according to the god. In the case that the global crisis is just impending, irrespective of their nationalities and races, the whole world should be strongly united to study measures in an effort to overcome it. The god says God will decide whether or not the asteroid really collides with the earth, after seeing the hearts of the people all over the world.

The Great East Japan Earthquake has hastened the probabilities of the predicted "Tokai earthquake," "Tonankai earthquake," and "Nankai earthquake." Furthermore, a god says that God will move forward the schedule of an earthquake with the center directly below the Metropolitan area. In the previous lectures, I relayed the message that a big earthquake hitting Japan's capital would never occur before the completion of TOKYO SKYTREE (completion in December, 2011; opening in spring, 2012). Due to the above-mentioned 3 earthquakes being scheduled earlier, however, I feel anxious about whether a massive earthquake hitting Tokyo will not really happen until the completion of TOKYO SKYTREE.

In fact, I received several messages from a god before the Great East Japan Earthquake.

On the morning of January 22 this year, I received a message from a god, and read it in from of about 500 people, as follows: "I want to say, 'A happy new year'; but we cannot take things so easily now. Many events are scheduled to take place this year, too. Thinking of this, we do not feel like cerebrating the new year without reserve."

Having this message early in a new year, I felt scared thinking about what's going to happen. Soon after that, Shinmoedake Volcano in Kyushu, the major southern island of Japan, erupted on January 6. Then, a god told me to change the hearts of the people for the better as soon as possible, which also urged me to update my blog more frequently.

Later, on February 2, a god said that such events that could stir up a sense of crisis would occur, including big earthquakes. He also mentioned that avian flu viruses would infect humans. Let me omit the details here, but I do hope you take a great care as human infection with bird flu viruses cannot be far away.

Since a new year, I have received a series of messages. Then, after a few months, on March 11, the Great East Japan Earthquake occurred.

In fact, I had a similar dream to my daughter's one on the

Epilogue: The time has come for the Japanese to be awaken to their mission

same day just before the Shinmoedake Volcano eruption. I was in Hiroshima Prefecture on my business trip, and my daughter was in Gifu Prefecture. When I said to her that I had a dream of an eruption of a volcano, she said that she had one in which a volcano erupted twice. "Having the same dream simultaneously may mean that an eruption can be realized in no time," I said to her. Surprisingly, two days after that, Shinmoedake Volcano erupted.

Before the Great East Japan Earthquake, I had a dream of an earthquake. It was at dawn on February 18. I stayed at a hotel in Tokyo to prepare for the Tokyo lecture coming on February 20.

In the dream, I saw an unfamiliar city. It was not such a big city as Tokyo but an urban city. The dream was too realistic, anyhow. With the jolt of the quake, glasses burst into pieces, making a snapping sound.

On the following day, I met the president and the executive managing director of a publishing firm to make arrangements over publishing my book, and inadvertently said to them: "I had a dream of an earthquake early in this morning. There may be an earthquake soon. As it was in an unfamiliar city, I guess it can't be a predicted powerful earthquake striking under the Tokyo Metropolitan area."

Then two days later, on February 22, a large-scale earthquake occurred in Christchurch in New Zealand, claiming many Japanese students' lives. Until then, I had believed that the place where a big earthquake occurred in my prophetic dream was New Zealand.

On March 11, however, I visited Tokyo again, and stayed the same hotel where I had had a dream of an earthquake. And there, I got caught in the Great East Japan Earthquake. I was on the 10th floor alone, and remembered the dream of an earthquake I had had in the same room before. Soon an idea flashed across my mind that the dream must have been exactly about the earthquake at that time. As the scale of an earthquake in the dream had been so huge that I got under the desk with my bag and cellphone immediately after I felt the jolt, anticipating the same scale earthquake as my dream.

The first one was a fearful rolling jolt, followed by a thrusting motion from below. I felt as if there had been so many earthquakes simultaneously. The powerful earthquake kept shaking for over 5 minutes, causing all drawers thrown open with the contents spilled on to the floor. Feeling that the quakes finally died away, I heard the bell of a fire escape and an emergency announcement over the hotel informing a fire.

Then I asked a god about the actions to take. He said: "Stay here. I will protect this room. This is the safest place." Following the advice, I decided to stay there. Soon after I felt the jolt, I tried to call my daughter and friends with my cellphone in vain.

Epilogue: The time has come for the Japanese to be awaken to their mission

A god at times told me that a natural calamity would start suddenly and unexpectedly; however, it came too sudden to be prepared. While the aftershocks continued to rattle Tokyo, I switched on TV from under the table. I will never ever forget the horrible scene of the tsunami jumping out of the screen. I could hardly bear to look at the dreadful sight.

"No wonder there will be another terrible natural disaster anytime and anywhere," a god says, "Plate motions and mantle convection currents have been activated, and now the whole world is approaching the period when huge earthquakes and violent eruptions of volcanoes are most likely to occur." The earth is a form of life; in other words, it is alive. Thus, the events of earthquakes and eruptions of volcanoes mean the self-defense of the earth, protecting itself from life-threatening conditions.

The Great East Japan Earthquake is said to have jolted areas, from the Prefecture of Hokkaido to Kagoshima Prefecture, almost all over Japan. Such a powerful earthquake is said to occur more frequently in future. Some places might be hit consecutively. These future earthquakes might drive Europe into a devastated situation; land might subside, and sunken islands might emerge, as seen in a god's message at the beginning of the epilogue. However, this is a current schedule based on people's minds, and may be changed by God.

As one of the best ways to notice gods' messages, I recommend you to look up at the sky. Prior to the Great East Japan Earthquake, a large number of earthquake cloud appeared. An earthquake cloud is seen before an earthquake occurs. On the morning of March 2, I saw an earthquake cloud, sharply extending from east to west, and I took a photo of that cloud. In the near future, an aurora could be visible, which is an uncommon natural phenomenon in Japan.

You should be cautious if you should see any sign of these phenomena in the sky, and also animals behaving unusually, because these are likely to be some messages or warnings from the earth.

I heard some people moved to somewhere deep in the mountains in Nagano Prefecture right after the Great East Japan Earthquake. Predicting the end of the current civilization, they seem to have started their new lives by digging caves in the mountains in order to prepare for that day. However, a god says: "It is totally wrong that they only think for themselves and try to survive. Those who think and live for others to the end will be able to survive at the end of this civilization."

You have nothing to be afraid of even if powerful earthquakes and natural disasters frequently take place. If you were to hear that this civilization would end tomorrow, I would like you to live even the last day as usual.

It is of prime importance to make efforts to live for others. Even if you eventually fail to live for others, gods are watching

Epilogue: The time has come for the Japanese to be awaken to their mission

you making strenuous efforts. "To try to do your best for others—this is the very beautiful aspect that humans are supposed to have, and deserves to be selected for the next civilization," a god says.

On the morning of the lecture in Tokyo, February 20, I watched a TV discussion on politics. I was wondering what would become of Japan while listening to their debate. Then I noticed a pretty great spirit in the studio through the screen. I asked a god who he was, and learned that he was Yoshida Shigeru, a former prime minister. He seemed anxious and furious about the politicians discussing on the program saying: "The present politicians are pathetic. What will become of Japan?" He just remained angry with them. The moment I thought it was an awkward situation, all the lights in the studio went off with a cracking sound, leaving the studio pitch dark. The lights in the studio rarely go off during a live broadcast. Later an emergency power source was switched on, and the debate continued in a dim lit studio. I think those who watched this program still remember this unusual event.

A god also thinks, "Japanese politicians should recognize that this is no time for pursuing party interests, since many people are suffering at this moment." This may be the reason why the lights went off in order to make them realize the current situation.

The Great East Japan Earthquake caused the Fukushima Dai-ichi nuclear plants to fall into a critical condition. A god has said for a long time that humans should not break down atoms or create cloned human beings. The rule that humans should never break down atoms in particular is stipulated in the rules of the universe.

This is not only the matter of nuclear power plants, but nuclear-powered submarines and nuclear missiles as well. As a result of breaking the rules of the universe and breaking down atoms, people have been facing the music of disaster of the Fukushima Dai-ichi nuclear plants. This is the work of gods aiming to discourage global pronuclear movements, starting from Japan.

That the atomic bombs dropped on Japan has a significant meaning. A god says that the place had to be Japan. Japan is a country of God, and that's why people in Japan were supposed to have the horrible experiences. Nevertheless, people have easily forgotten the fear, continuously breaking down atoms without realizing its sin, seeking after convenience and desire, eventually developing the current flourishing civilization. If people had recognized gods' intension at the time of the atomic bombings, and had decided not to introduce any nuclear in Japan, the Fukushima nuclear plants disaster would never have occurred.

Epilogue: The time has come for the Japanese to be awaken to their mission

Japanese had been persuaded into believing that nuclear fuel was safe, which led the whole nation to develop nuclear plants so far. The safety myth of nuclear plants, however, simply lost all credibility due to this accident of the Fukushima Dai-ichi nuclear plants. Unless people repent of their errors of having broken atoms, there will be another nuclear accident in the near future.

It is indeed true that one of the goals of nuclear promotion is to reduce carbon dioxide emission. With the best use of Japan's state-of-the-art technology, however, alternative energy from natural resources could meet our electricity demands. As we will have more windy days due to global warming, expectations for wind power generation will increase.

Of course there are many that each of us can do. We can reduce energy consumption by carefully saving electricity and changing our life style, albeit with a little inconvenience.

I hope people do not take this Fukushima nuclear accident so negatively, because you may be protected by gods if you seriously repent of our errors of having broken down atoms. You will be able to protect yourself by reflecting on yourself with a pure heart, having close ties with gods and with fortune favoring you.

Here is a message I received from a god in February, 2010.

A message from a god

*For the last several months, in the sea (the Sea of Japan) of
the Hokuriku Region, the illusory huge fish
have been springing up in rapid succession.
The huge fish, with a name given by humans,
live deep in the sea at a depth of 200 to 1,000 meters,
and are most unlikely to be found, only once in 10 years or so.
However, for the past one month and a half,
only in Ishikawa Prefecture, as many as 14 cases
have been reported that such rare fish were washed ashore.
It is not the kind of thing that this unusual event was only due
to the change of the ocean current.
Global warming has been rapidly raising the temperature of not
only the global surface but also the sea bottom.
People are astonished to accidentally find a large number of fish
dead at the seashore, but it is only a portion.
A number of deep-sea fish were killed because of the increase of
the sea-bottom temperature and poisonous gases,
and quite a few of them were left dead on the seabed.
We gave some warnings to human beings
when a huge number of ayu or sweetfish were found dead
floating on the Nagara River
and also when tadpoles and small fish fell out of the sky.*

Epilogue: The time has come for the Japanese to be awaken to their mission

*However, many people have hardly noticed them.
When the summer is drawing near,
there will be small-scale tornados,
and also tadpoles and small fish will fall from the sky again,
which will lead to a warning of a full-scale tornado.
The fact that the illusory huge fish have been utterly exhausted
and eventually found dead
upon reaching the beach one after another,
is attributed to magmatic activation . . .
That is, we warn you
that it will not be long before another big earthquake occurs.
Great slides of the tectonic plates at the bottom of the Japan Sea
will cause a violent jolt in the vicinity.
You should not lightly take events and small changes
that take place around you.
You should not pass over unusual occurrences,
such as marine creatures' (seals, shark, and other fish)
unusually straying into rivers, a plague of insects,
creatures' moving their habitats, and their massive deaths.
You should also take these things as an omen of a cataclysm.
And then, you should be appropriately prepared for that
(mental preparation, saving for emergency, evacuation drill,
and discussion with the people around you).
Mental preparation does not only mean
to prepare for extraordinary natural disasters,*

but to change yourself by reflecting on your errors
and making your heart clean and pure,
so that you will be good enough
to survive any powerful earthquake.
In addition, you should continuously pass on this message
to your family, friends, and anyone around you.
Your efforts and contribution to people
will prolong this civilization still further.
In other words,
you will be given a little more time for saving people.

I read this message at each of our lectures held in 2010. "Such natural disasters as earthquakes, tornados, and large-scale typhoons are to take place in the vicinity of nuclear power plants in the near future, in order to discourage the Japanese, who have taken up a special mission, from repeating sins," says a god.

In this message, the possibility of an earthquake on the coast of the Japan Sea is also mentioned. In Fukui Prefecture, there are 14 nuclear reactors, including the suspended ones, the largest number in Japan. Therefore, if the same scale of an earthquake as the Great East Japan Earthquake occurs in the vicinity of Fukui Prefecture, its damage would be much more than the Fukushima Dai-ichi nuclear disaster. Just imagining the situation makes me feel scary. I am concerned that there

Epilogue: The time has come for the Japanese to be awaken to their mission

may be another tragedy unless the Japanese seriously reflect on having broken down atoms and push for a nonnuclear future.

In our lecture held in Hiroshima Prefecture on March 20, 2011, a god said: "Radioactive leakage in the earth will cause damage to other planets. Extraterrestrial Intelligence is currently paying attention to the Fukushima Dai-ichi nuclear plant. UFOs will be seen in the sky in the near future." Later, as the god mentioned, UFOs have been frequently seen around the Fukushima Dai-ichi nuclear plant. If this trend continues, humans will eventually contaminate not only the earth but also other planets. As a result, the earth will get bashed by other planets, which could endanger the existence of the earth, a living organism. If so, our earth would never be able to be recovered. That's why I really want everyone to humbly reconsider your conduct. Thus, I would like to continuously call for this message to everyone through our lectures. If you attend our lectures and feel something, share the message with the people around you accordingly, because it is your mission as a messiah, a savior.

I will conclude this book with the two messages from a god. The first one is what I received on July 18, 2007, and the second on October 8, 2010, respectively.

A message from a god

*As previously announced, the earth has started to shake.
From now on until an eruption of Mt. Fuji,
there will be earthquakes across Japan
and the damage will be inevitable.
As some earthquakes will occur
in the place you can never expect,
many seismologists will get confused.
Earthquakes will take place not only in Japan,
but the whole world will face natural disasters,
such as earthquakes, hurricanes, growing typhoons
and frequent tornados.
There will be no end to the number of the victims.
The day will come when human beings shiver with fear.
You must reap what you have sown.
Human beings have broken one of the rules of the universe,
placing too much confidence in their capabilities.
Breaking down atoms is
what human beings should never ever do,
and has been believed to lead you down the path of destruction.
Ignoring our warning, you have continuously broken down
atoms (development of nuclear energy and nuclear capacity).
Everything is integrated.*

Epilogue: The time has come for the Japanese to be awaken to their mission

All things in the universe are connected.
Even a single fragment cannot be separated from all the others.
Inside the earth is now screaming. You should listen to its cry.
After a while, human beings are supposed to pay the penalty
in the form of natural disasters
(with disappointment rather than anger).
You should realize how incapable
and small you, human beings are,
admit the seriousness of what you have done,
such as the destruction of nature and environmental pollution,
and reflect humbly on yourselves.
Then, you should apologize to God for having destroyed
the earth too badly to inhabit anymore.
Nothing can be done by the powerless human beings.
Leave the following matters up to God,
and obediently lend God a helping hand.
Did you get it?

A message from a god

No matter what may happen in the future,
never fail to remember that you are connected with God
who created this world, furthermore, the universe.
Be aware that you are inseparably bound up with this universe.

"This universe" does not mean only the galactic system,
but also the extragalactic universe.
Within your limited knowledge,
you believe this whole galactic system is the universe,
and try to explore the unknown world by launching rockets
to only a part of the limited space of the universe.
No matter how much time and money human beings may spend
on the search for the space by launching rockets,
it is absolutely impossible to probe the whole universe.
Do you know why?
It is because you have physical bodies.
Since you exist in the 3-dimensional space,
many of your souls with physical bodies are not allowed
to travel to the farthest corner of the universe,
with the exception of those who have acquired
the knack of dimensional crossover.
With the senses of human beings with physical bodies,
this space expands overwhelmingly indefinitely.
There are stars visible to the naked eye in this space,
but let's suppose you could go forward farther and farther.
If you continuously moved on
spending hundreds of millions of light-years,
you would return to the original place again.
As you see, the universe is a sphere.
Outside of the sphere, the even farther universe lies there,

Epilogue: The time has come for the Japanese to be awaken to their mission

where there exist advanced stars.
(Let me put this way now.)
Your destination will be the world of light.
You will be one of the beings of light.
Now you are one of such beings
as to have physical bodies and souls.
You might feel lonely, incredible, or hard to accept the reality
when you leave your physical bodies
(to become the beings without physical bodies).
However, you do not have to worry about, because
the world of light is a supremely wonderful world.
As we have mentioned many times,
the time has come for the earth to evolve,
which does not mean that the earth itself will disappear,
but will change greatly for the better.
The balance of force and location, which leads to
magnetic force (the earth itself possesses it) and gravity,
will change (a change of the earth's axial tilt).
This variation of the earth's axial tilt
will change the length of the current 24-hour day,
taking away the present time interval.
Those who will be able to move on
to the new earth (the earth reborn) with your physical bodies,
may have a strange feeling for a while.
There is nothing to worry about.

You will soon get used, and adjust yourselves,
to new circumstances.
You deserve to live in the new earth.
However, you need physical strength to some extent.
You should gain strength.
Purify your spirits, hearts, and bodies.
A wonderful future is ahead of you.

Afterword

I would like to express sincere thanks for reading through this book.

In asking a god for advice regarding the title, I received a message that I should put the title, "Salvation Through Yourself." The god also mentioned that I should ask each reader to be a savior who can save precious, and loved, ones.

In this book, as well as in the previous one *WATARASE: The way to your higher self*, I have written about the importance of purifying our mind. However hard I try to share my feeling, your family and friends around you will believe what you say better than what I write.

I think you read through this book in order to save the people around you—that is, those who cannot be saved without you, and those with the souls deeply connected with yours.

I do hope the readers of this book will save people. What help should be offered, however, depends on each of you. A god says: "You do not have to feel pressure with my desire to you to be a savior. The readers of this book can save people in a natural flow." That's why, I think, you encountered this book.

"Then, what can I do?" some people might think. For instance, you can lend this book to your friends and let them read it in turn, or read my blog and recommend it to your friends.

And also I would like you to encourage the people around you to join our Miracle Lectures as I mentioned in Chapter 2. Attending our Miracle Lectures will change your consciousness for the better. People's enhanced consciousness will enable us to escape with a small misfortune instead of a possible calamity in the future. This is the reason I would like as many people as possible to join the lectures.

I found something amazing through publishing books and writing my blog. My books and blog have been emitting the power of the universe, and I have already received a lot of reports of miraculous experiences. The details will be included in my next book.

It is never a coincidence that you read this book. I do hope to see you someday somewhere. I am really looking forward to the day.

Kazuyo Omori
May, 2011

Author Profile

Kazuyo Omori
Born in Gifu Prefecture in Japan, she has had spiritual powers since her childhood, and receives direct guidance from God and other deities.
She has had multitudes of mysterious and mystical experiences, including premonitions of the future, an encounter with a huge UFO, out-of-body experiences (or astral projection), and conversations with deities and other spirits. She currently puts her remarkable abilities to work through her activities as a spiritual counselor.
Now she is traveling all over Japan to participate in lectures as a guest in order to spread many messages she has received from deities. Among those who have attended these lectures, there have been multitudes of miraculous experiences, including physical healing, and more and more people are coming back to the lectures all the time.

The number of visitors to her hot and mysterious blog "WATARASE-masse!!" has grown sharply, too. Here she provides comfort, warmth, and cheer to her readers, who receive the power of the universe just by reading it, and she continually hears from individuals who have had miraculous results from doing so.
(http://ameblo.jp/oomori-kazuyo/)

Furthermore, she has her own radio program *We are always connected! WATARASE Talk.* In this program, she provides the heartwarming messages to her listeners.
Each episode of this program is available as a YouTube video with English subtitles.
http://www.youtube.com/user/officewatarase/

Literary work: *WATARASE: The way to your higher self* (Tama Publishing)

Salvation Through Yourself　WATARASE Vol. 2

2013年10月10日　初版第1刷発行

著　者　Kazuyo Omori
発行者　韮澤 潤一郎
発行所　株式会社 たま出版
　　　　〒160-0004 東京都新宿区四谷4-28-20
　　　　　　☎ 03-5369-3051（代表）
　　　　　　http://tamabook.com
　　　　　　振替　00130-5-94804

印刷所　株式会社エーヴィスシステムズ

©Kazuyo Omori 2013　Printed in Japan
ISBN978-4-8127-0360-1　C0011